GATHERING

Gathering

Memoir *of a* Seed Saver

DIANE OTT WHEALY

Library of Congress Control Number: 2011925379

Publisher's Cataloging-in-Publication Data
Ott Whealy, Diane.
Gathering : memoir of a seed saver / Diane Ott Whealy.
p. cm.
ISBN: 978-0-615-45774-1
1. Conservationists—United States—Biography.
2. Gene banks, Plant—United States.   I. Title.
QH31.O87 2011
333.72'092—dc22   2011925379

Front illustration: *Moon and Stars Watermelon with
Eastern Tiger Salamander* by Judith Ann Griffith

PRODUCED BY WILSTED & TAYLOR PUBLISHING SERVICES
Project manager Christine Taylor
Designer and compositor Yvonne Tsang
Proofreader Melody Lacina
Indexer Andrew Joron
Color supervisor Susan Schaefer
Printer's devil Lillian Marie Wilsted
Printer Friesens Corporation

Printed in Canada

SEED SAVERS EXCHANGE
3094 North Winn Road
Decorah, Iowa 52101
www.seedsavers.org

Dedicated to past generations,
the noble guardians who have
cared for our seed heritage,
and to my grandsons,
Jack, Owen, Grant,
and Solomon,
the future.

CONTENTS

Acknowledgments ix

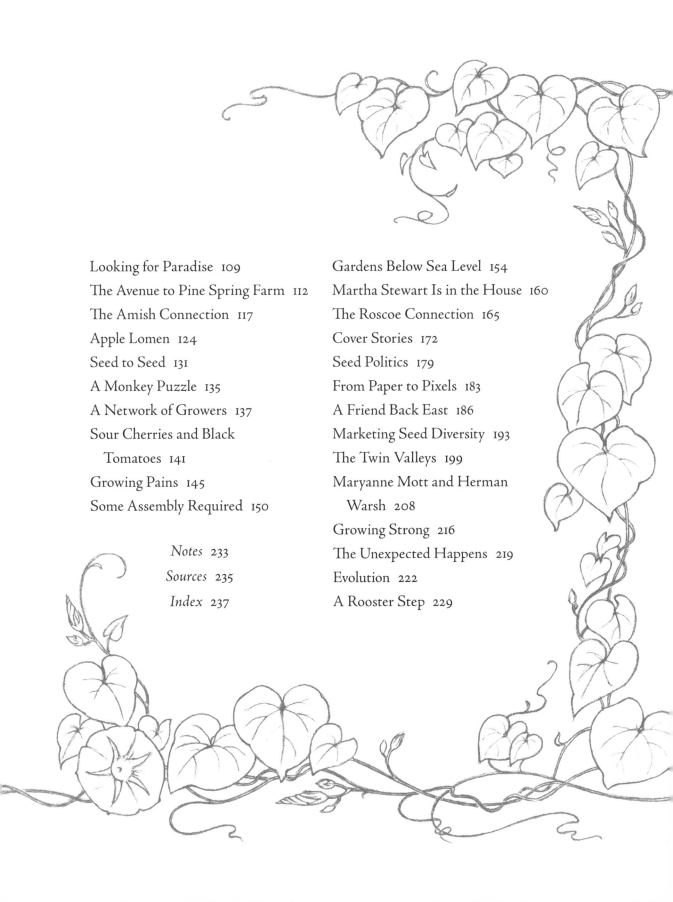

ACKNOWLEDGMENTS

This book is a gathering of people, seeds, and stories. Although it would be impossible to thank everyone who contributed to the success of Seed Savers Exchange over the last thirty-six years, and to this book in particular, my deepest gratitude for their support and inspiration goes to my grandparents; my parents, Fidelis and Helen Ott; and my children, Aaron, Amy, Tracy, Carrie, and Jessica. My children's partners—Becky Whaley, Adam Miller, Ryan Heryford, and Dylan Stoen—as well as other family members, including Robert Ott, Kathy Humpal, Aunt Hermina Koudelka, and Floyd and Laurie Ott, were also sources of support. I relied on the kindness of many friends, members, associates, and benefactors, including Maryanne Mott, Greg Brown, Tim and Jennifer Cantine, Jerry and Patti Johnson, Linda Watson, Glenn and Linda Drowns, Suzanne Ashworth, Will Bonsall, Gary Nabhan, Clarice Cooper, Tom and Sue Knoche, Dan Bussey, Arllys and Lorado Adelmann, Kevin and Leslie Sand, John Swenson, Jim Henry, David Sliwa, Kurt Baucum, Becky Silva, Wes Jackson, Dana Jackson, Jamie and Susan Banks, Tom Goodmann, Wayne Wangsness, Wes Henthorne, Marty Teitel, Mark Kane, Deborah Madison, and the late Barbara Robinette Moss. I am also grateful to my neighbors Garry and Judy Cox, Ronna and Jackie Clapham, Melvin and Sue Stouts, Robert and Phyllis Kauffman, Charlie and

Val Cunningham, Herb Ehrie, Dave Schmidt, Karen Bauman, Bill McLain, and Herb, Betty, and Mark Covey. And I thank my former husband, Kent Whealy, co-founder of Seed Savers Exchange, whose vision, fortitude, and enthusiasm—especially during those precarious early years—gave our organization the strength to grow.

Cass Peterson Doolittle and other patient editors all wielded the pruning shears with sensitivity, and generously guided and encouraged me. The staff at Seed Savers Exchange, especially Joanne Thuente, Bill Musser, Shannon Carmody, and John Torgrimson, lent their professional expertise.

Judith Ann Griffith contributed her exquisite illustrations, and many photographers shared historic images that chronicle the growth of Seed Savers Exchange over the years. Thanks are owed to Christine Taylor and her associates at Wilsted and Taylor Publishing Services for designing and producing such a beautiful book.

My heartfelt thanks go to George D. DeVault, former Executive Director of Seed Savers Exchange, who recognized how important it was for me to tell the story of Seed Savers Exchange in my own words. He and his wife, Melanie DeVault, gave me the courage to get started. I am indebted to the Board of Directors of Seed Savers Exchange for their faith in me: Amy P. Goldman, Neil Hamilton, Rob Johnston Jr., Cary Fowler, Rosalind Creasy, Keith Crotz, David Cavagnaro, Glenn Drowns, Larry Grimstad, and George DeVault. They are as committed to preserving the founding spirit of Seed Savers Exchange as they are to preserving our treasure trove of garden seeds for future generations.

Henry David Thoreau once said, "If you have built castles in the air, your work need not be lost; that is where they should be. Now put the foundations under them." My eternal gratitude to everyone who helped build that foundation.

GATHERING

Going Down to Grandpa's

I grew up knowing that you harvest horseradish only in months with an "r" in them and that every day gets a "rooster step" longer after the shortest day of the year. My life has always been connected to growing things, for food or beauty, and telling stories about them. So it was natural that I grew to adulthood fascinated by and comfortable with people, seeds, and the environment.

In 1884, my great-grandparents, Michael and Margaret Ertl Ott, emigrated from Dreuschendorf, Germany, to a farm about five miles from St. Lucas, a German settlement in the northeast corner of Iowa. They built a log cabin east of town, where my grandfather, Baptist John Ott, and his ten brothers and sisters were born. My grandfather purchased sixty acres from his father when he married my grandmother, Helena Rose Hackman, in 1916.

A generation later, when I was a child, Dad would often come into the house after milking and say, "We should go down to Grandpa's tonight and see how they're doing." On summer evenings, after supper, we'd drive to my grandparents' farm, about five miles southwest of our home near Festina, Iowa. Gurgle Hill—also known as Lovers' Lane—was our favorite shortcut. It was a narrow trail that passed by several abandoned farmsteads, and my big brother, Bob, and I loved to hear our parents' stories about who used to live there.

TOP: Baptist John and Helena Hackman Ott
on their wedding day, May 9, 1916
ABOVE: Grandma and Grandpa Ott
fifty-some years later

"That's where the old Bengfort farm was, not much left now," one or the other would say. "That farm was always perfect, the lawn mowed and never a weed on the place. I remember driving by this time of day and his cows would look so contented in the pasture, and now the barn is all but gone. Not much left of the farm anymore, just the windmill, some old stone foundations, apple and plum trees still standing in the yard. I wonder what happened to his workhorses? They were old Henny Bengfort's pride and joy."

Past the Bengfort farm, we drove down a hill and over a creaky wooden bridge. "There's the waterfall!" I'd shout, and my brother and I would try to be the first to spot water gushing from a hillside in the pasture.

On those early evening drives, Mom would tell stories about growing up. "Joe Etteldorf from town owned about twenty acres over there, where he kept his horses and calves in the summer. When I was a child, we'd walk past the meadow on our way to go fishing. I'll never forget the day we saw horses drinking from the waterfall!"

Next came a house shaded by a perfect maple tree. In the fall the tree glowed brilliant orange. I was sure my dad would say: "When I was growing up, the daughter of the people who lived there died in her sleep in the bedroom upstairs. They never did find out why." I would try to get that image out of my head right away.

The path wound through a shallow creek by the Dietzenbach place. Dad drove slowly downhill and into the water, then speeded up to reach the other side. A gravel road continued, with the Little Turkey River on one side and fields of corn, in the summertime taller than our car, on the other. After winding past the wall of corn, the road twisted up Bass Creek Hill, to Grandpa's sawmill and their house.

Grandpa and Grandma Ott first lived in a small log cabin where the windmill now stands. My father was born in that cabin in 1920. In 1921, Grandpa built the four-bedroom, two-story farmhouse that's still there today.

The house, painted white, sat in the middle of an amazing yard. Four Seven Sisters roses were planted on the edge of the lawn, where the sidewalk to the house began. Grandma Ott loved those ramblers, which bore trusses of flowers that opened dark magenta and gradually lightened to shell pink, making it look as if there were seven colors of roses on one plant. She always wanted us to stop, admire, and smell those roses.

Grandpa claimed to be mystified about why she liked them so much, complaining that the branches were "so gosh darn stickery." No one took him seriously. We knew he was the greatest admirer of all.

The back yard along the road was enclosed with large cedars transplanted from the neighbor's woods, and lilac bushes in front of chestnut trees. Peonies grew in several places in the yard. Hollyhocks and sunflowers were planted around the outhouse, their tall stalks helping to camouflage the outdoor toilet.

Grandma planted geraniums—overwintered each year in big pails by the kitchen woodstove—along the south side of the house. In the flower beds on the north side were dahlias. Grandpa said he never

Grandpa Ott's
morning glory

liked the dahlias, which grew so tall they had to be staked. He took pride in his morning glories, which grew on the east side of the porch. Every year he would train the vine's heart-shaped leaves up a twine trellis on the side of the porch. Grandma, not to be outdone by Grandpa's perennial complaints about the dahlias, said the morning glories were "just flycatchers in the fall. If they weren't so pretty I would never plant them."

In the summer, their porch, enclosed with a wall of morning glories, felt like a special outdoor room, safe and cozy, and a wonderful place to sit and listen to my grandparents' stories.

Every year, just before I went back to school, I'd help Grandpa pluck seedpods off the vine. The pods turned beige when they were ripe, and we'd put them into small glass jars before they burst onto the ground. We knew that enough seed would fall from the vines to self-sow. But just to be sure, Grandpa saved extra seed to be planted the next year, or to give to visitors who admired those deep purple blossoms. Before long, the entire community was sprouting with Grandpa Ott's morning glories.

As I helped him in the garden, it never occurred to me that I was doing anything out of the ordinary, or that the simple act of saving those seeds would one day describe my life's work.

Homegrown

Grandpa's nickname was Bob Ott, and he was a legend for various reasons throughout eastern Iowa. Even today if you mention his name, some colorful stories will be forthcoming. I thought my grandpa could do anything. He was a self-taught veterinarian who apprenticed by going on sick calls with a vet from the next county. Grandpa stitched up his own cuts, and delivered all ten of his children.

He owned a sawmill with his neighbor Carl Baumler, had a cream route, was a blacksmith, operated a still, knew the best spot in the woods to harvest ginseng, and worked as a bouncer at all the local wedding dances. He was known for drinking beer and playing cards at Klemer's Tavern in St. Lucas, and for getting into fights. He was also fond of fishing for carp with the local priest, Father Schuh. Grandpa made a special carp bait with cornmeal and warm water, wrapped in a cotton ball. The carp were destined for the smokehouse. (Smoked carp is still popular in snack stands along the Mississippi.)

Grandma conceded, in her quiet voice, that "after a few beers Grandpa could be hard to live with." She deserved to be canonized Saint Helena, patron saint of patience, for living with Grandpa and raising their nine children during the Great Depression. (They lost their daughter Agnes to whooping cough at two months, though her twin, Leo, survived.)

Grandpa was a large man, three hundred pounds at his prime. On workdays, he wore a blue denim shirt with Big Smith striped overalls. During the summer, he rolled up his shirtsleeves to show a tattoo of an American eagle under a waving banner, acquired at the Dairy Cattle Congress in Waterloo, Iowa, years before.

On Sundays, he wore a black suit to church, and for other special occasions he wore his overalls, but with a crisp white shirt. He carried a pack of Lucky Strikes and a book of matches in his left front pocket. A brass snap closed his right pocket, which held a profusion of important papers along with his billfold, thick with $100 bills (friends and neighbors often borrowed money from him). Between the pockets was a narrow compartment where he kept a carpenter pencil.

Grandpa was very strict, his voice stern and loud. "When he said something we would pay attention," my father told me. "He wouldn't have to say it twice."

He spoke Low Dutch, High Dutch, and broken English—and swore in all three languages. His Belgian workhorses—Guy, Charlie, Dewey, and Lady—obeyed his German commands. I watched many afternoons as Grandpa went through the gate by the barn, heading back to do field work or fix fence. I never understood what Grandpa said, but the horses did and followed his orders to go forward, back up, or stop. My grandfather farmed only with horses, and I remember the day my parents sold their workhorses, Dewey and Dick. It was around 1957—long after most farmers had gone to powered equipment.

On visits to Grandpa and Grandma, we headed for the gardens first. There was a warm spot on the south side of the hog barn where lettuce, radishes, spinach, peas, new potatoes, beets, onions, and carrots were planted in long rows, perfectly straight and free of weeds. One shorter row was reserved for the seed of German Pink tomato, kohlrabi, and cabbage. When the seedlings were large enough to move to their own row in the garden, they were set out in the early morning after a rain, and covered at night with coffee cans to keep them warm.

The hill above the barn, where the soil was sandier, provided a home for watermelons, along with pie pumpkins that would be put in the cellar to store over the winter. On the edge of the cornfield behind the barn were rows of sweet corn and "pickles," as we called cucumbers. Green beans and navy beans grew in front. At the end of that garden was a small orchard of Wealthy apple and Whitney crabapple trees, with rhubarb and chives growing between them: a glorious place to play.

A spot by the machine shed was reserved for the potato patch. When my father was growing up, it was large enough to feed the whole family through the year. "I remember digging potatoes was a major job," he recalls. "All those rows seemed like there was no end and it was always hot. We dug with forks and put the potatoes in small piles to dry. We'd pick up pails and pails and pour the potatoes into the 'single box' wagon. Ma sorted them and set aside the small ones to boil with their skins for fried potatoes. Nice ones were kept in a gunnysack in the basement to plant the next year. The rest went into the bin. We'd get one of the horses, pull the wagon up to the house, and unload the potatoes down a chute that Pa made right into the basement."

Copenhagen Market cabbage

As I got older, I appreciated even more the way my grandparents provided for themselves and their children. The gardens were vital to sustaining a large family. Grandma Ott's grocery list for Perry's Store in St. Lucas consisted of flour, sugar, coffee, salt, and spices, and she took a gallon jug to the store to be filled with brown vinegar from a wooden barrel. The rest of their food came from what their hands and land produced, and a bountiful crop was a measure of their success.

Store-bought seed, like store-bought anything else, was a luxury. So they saved seed from year to year, as their parents and their parents' parents had. Grandma saved seeds from watermelons, pumpkins, beans, corn, melons, and tomatoes. She bought only what she couldn't easily save—the seeds of biennial vegetables, for instance, like carrot, cabbage, and kohlrabi. But she still loved to pore through seed catalogs and dream about someday ordering more. Aunt Hermina told me her mother reacted with delight when the seed catalogs arrived: "Ma's face would light up and she'd rub her hands together, so anxious to start looking through those colorful pages of Henry Field's and Gurney's. She would spend hours reading and deciding."

My parents had a wonderful garden, too, but that one seemed slightly less magical to me, perhaps because I had to hoe long rows of potatoes and corn, or sit with my brother on the front porch, shelling washtubs of peas for Mom to freeze. Just as we thought we could almost see the bottom of the tub, Mom brought another pail. I feared we would never be finished, and I didn't even like peas. My grandparents' gardens seemed like Eden. Our garden seemed like work.

After our garden tours at Grandma and Grandpa's, we would sit outside on metal lawn chairs while my parents and grandparents chatted. I felt satisfied, listening to the grown-ups' voices in the warm evening air. Sometimes, from the pasture, we heard a quail calling out a perfectly clear "bobwhite." If the weather wasn't good we would head up to the porch, where the morning glories climbed. Grandpa left an opening in the vines each year—a square, a circle, or a rectangle— so we could watch the cars go by. He knew everyone driving on the road and usually had a comment: "Wonder where she's going. Don't they ever stay home?" or "He's late for milking again!"

When the lightning bugs started blinking, it was time to go inside. We sat in the living room and the conversations could get loud. Grandpa had a pin in his leg, the result of a car accident when he was sixty-three, and sat on the couch with his leg propped up. A cane he'd made from ironwood rested by his hand. I never walked by the couch for fear he might decide to catch my leg with his cane.

Grandpa and Grandma had a large walnut wardrobe in their bedroom. On the top shelf, Grandpa kept a brown paper bag filled with root beer barrels, jawbreakers, and other penny candy. My brother, Bob, younger sister, Kathy, and I listened to the conversations, the clock ticking on the library table, and the screeching of Grandma's hearing aid. Eventually Grandpa got up off the couch, made his way to the bedroom, and returned with a fistful of candy, several pieces for each of us.

Around 10 o'clock, Dad would remark, "Well, it's time to head for the hills." That was Grandma's signal to say, "I'll make lunch quick." Lunch was any meal between breakfast, dinner, and supper. Even at 10 o'clock in the evening, it was expected that we would have lunch before we went home.

Soon you could smell the coffee boiling on the stove in the kitchen. Grandpa would get out some homemade wurst—he did his own butchering and smoked the sausage himself—and mix horseradish with vinegar, cream, and sugar. Bread went on a plate, and butter in a round dish. He opened a jar of "1-2-3 pickles" and a pint of "huckleberry smear" or ground-cherry jam. Grandma was the best baker, and we always had a sweet dessert. My favorite was apple pie made with the windfalls from the Wealthy apple tree. Of course the piecrust was made with lard. In the winter, we might eat canned whole crabapples or plum sauce with cream. Grandma had a cut-glass berry bowl with matching smaller bowls that she used for her canned blackcap berry sauce.

Grandma was as gentle as Grandpa was brusque. She always wore a print dress and an apron made from cotton feed sacks and trimmed with rickrack, with pockets for her rosary and handkerchief. She loved her everyday dishes, ordered with coupons from Gold Medal flour sacks. The dishes were white, with scalloped edges, and looked pretty next to the red-handled flatware.

After the table was set and all the food put out, the rest of us went into the kitchen, with its soft blue walls and pine floors that creaked. I always tried to sit beside Grandma, who sat below a beautiful picture with the words "God Bless Our Home" surrounded by orange flowers inside a thick gold frame. Grandma poured coffee for everyone, including the children, before she sat down.

Sometimes Grandma would hand us a small bag of Whitney crab-apples or cookies on our way out the door. In the dark, we drove home on a better road than the one we came on. We crossed the sturdy bowstring iron bridge, the timber stringers clapping behind us. I could still smell the coffee on my blouse and hear Grandpa Ott's voice.

The Home Place

Festina is in a rural corner of Iowa, settled by families who emigrated from Germany and never left. Small dairy farms were passed down from generation to generation. As a child, I felt as if my corner of Iowa was about ten years behind most of the country and at least twenty years behind California. The rest of the world was like another planet.

My parents' farm was called "the home place" because it was where my mother, Helen, was born and where her parents, Joseph and Catherine Einck, had farmed. One day I heard a neighbor ask my dad, "How big is your farm, Dale?" My dad said, "Well, it was one hundred acres until they paved the Number 11, the old blacktop, and put Highway 150 in and the county took five acres." He seemed bothered, but I thought our farm was just big enough.

My brother and sister and I knew every inch of that land. We knew where all the cow paths were in the pasture, and even where Grandpa Einck had buried a horse when my mother was young. We knew where to find arrowheads and where the old wooden buggies and farm machinery ended up. I knew where the gooseberry and "stuckleberry" bushes were, and where black raspberries could be found at the edge of the woods. In the spring I knew where to find buttercups, bluebells, and a hillside covered with purple phlox. There were wild rose bushes and plum trees, and the pasture was full of hickory, butternut, and black walnut trees. We knew all the springs that fed the creek, where we went to wade in the deep holes and dig gray clay from the banks. And we knew when to pick the wild strawberries that grew on the cool side of the creek bank.

Pasture ditches, in rural Iowa, were the equivalent of modern

Diane and her father
and brother, Bob,
June 1954

landfills, the final resting place of old cast-iron stoves, scrap metal, machinery, and cars. A favorite of ours was Scheidel's Ditch, a ravine where all the neighbors threw their junk. We never knew what we'd find—an old bicycle, toys, or other treasures for my playhouse. We often took our BB guns and shot at bottles we'd lined up against the side of the ditch.

But Bob and I also had chores. Every day we had to make sure the cows were home before the evening milking. We started calling them from the barn about 4:30 in the afternoon: "Come boss, come boss!" On hot summer days we hoped our voices would be enough to bring the cows in. Sometimes they would start to head back, but usually they didn't want to leave their grass any sooner than necessary. After much yelling, my brother and I would go down in the pasture and bring them home. When the cows saw us coming, they lined up, always in the same order. The leader was Annabelle, followed by Rose. They took a one-lane cow path back to the barn, crossing the creek at the same place every day, and always stopped for a drink. Each cow knew which stanchion was hers and courteously entered the barn in the right order.

After the evening milking, we would let the cows into their night pasture, a small meadow between two grassed hills south of the barn, so that they would be close for the morning milking. Many summer evenings our whole family would sit on the grassy hillside, looking for four-leaf clovers and watching the cows contentedly graze.

The farm had many small crop fields, each with its own name. When Dad left after dinner, I would hear him tell Mom what field he'd be in that afternoon. "Diane can bring lunch," Mom sometimes said. Hearing that I would take lunch—the mid-afternoon meal, not to be confused with the midday dinner—was good news. Around 3 o'clock, Dad would stop plowing, turn off the tractor, and wait for me at the end of the field.

Mom often made extra so I could eat lunch with Dad. She packed it in the same aluminum kettle she used for gathering eggs or for cooking a dozen or so ears of fresh corn on the cob. It had a smooth wire handle with a small wooden spool to grip for carrying. She lined the kettle with a white cotton feed sack, folding it over the food. Dad might get two fried egg sandwiches on homemade bread, wrapped in waxed paper, and I'd get a smaller sandwich.

Almost every afternoon, Mom baked cookies, cake, or pies. It was never a problem to find something sweet to pack with the egg sand-wiches. On hot days, Mom would send along a quart jar of cold water, and every day there was hot coffee.

Fried egg sandwiches, fresh cookies, and coffee . . . I would find Dad and we would sit under a tree at the end of the field and eat lunch. We didn't talk, but those were the best afternoons of the summer.

Seeing the World

In June 1968, five teenaged girls took a train from Marion, Iowa, to Denver, Colorado. Destination: Estes Park. I was eighteen years old, newly graduated from De Sales High School in Ossian, and felt the need to explore. It was a time of disillusionment; three heroes had been lost—President Jack Kennedy, his brother Bob, and the Reverend Martin Luther King Jr. And as my grandmother would put it, I wanted to fly the coop.

Once on the train, we didn't look back. We were comfortable heading to Colorado, with no job or place to stay. The spirit of exploration and the lack of doubt that I could do whatever it took to survive was in my DNA. But perhaps unlike those ancestors who boarded a ship to America in 1884, I was expecting to have fun.

When the train arrived in Denver, we decided to take a cab to Estes Park. The cab driver at first laughed at the idea, but he must have felt our excitement and wanted to come along on our ride for a while. He agreed to take us, charging only for the gas, and called his office to announce that he wouldn't be back for the rest of the day. We stopped at a diner in Loveland for breakfast, and arrived in Estes Park early in the afternoon. After storing our bags at the bus station, we began to explore this small village nestled into a narrow valley in the Rocky Mountains, with the Big Thompson River flowing right through the middle.

I had never seen anything so magnificent as the mountains. When I got out of the car, the air smelled like pure happiness. Within days we had found a place to rent, a small cabin above the police station on Virginia Street (it was called the Du Kum Inn), and we all had jobs. Mae Jean worked at a food stand along the main street, Highway 34, and came home smelling of hot dogs. Linda worked at Hart's Buffeteria; Patti worked at the Edelweiss House, selling lederhosen. Jeannie and I were waitresses at the Coffee Bar, a café where we met local residents and vacationing families.

We all moonlighted, working the dinner shift at the Plantation Restaurant, across the street from the Coffee Bar. We wore gold ruffled headbands and shiny uniforms with aprons. The Burgess brothers, Tom and Bill, owned the restaurant. Tom baked pies and Bill was the businessman. We lived for the strawberry rhubarb pie and soon knew how to debone rainbow trout at the table.

But I disappointed my parents when they came to visit that summer. As a parochial school student, I had gone to church every day for twelve years, and every Sunday in summer. My mother, arriving in Estes Park, asked, "Where is the Catholic church?" I didn't have a clue!

Diane and St. Bernard puppy on Twin Sisters Peak, Estes Park, Colorado, 1970

Maybe that explains what I wasn't doing. Instead, we hitchhiked everywhere, hosted parties, smoked but (just in case we ever ran for public office) refrained from inhaling. We hiked but never conquered Long's Peak; we spent our days waitressing and lying in the sun, and after work we went to bars. Jax Snax was our favorite. It had a band every night, and we loved to dance. The side door was always open to the Big Thompson River, and we would sit on boulders in the moonlight, watching the icy water crash down from the mountains.

Farther along the street was the Wheel Bar, family-owned and -operated since 1945 and in all those years open every day but Christmas. Its motto was "Help Stamp Out Thirst! Drink at the Wheel!"

The most memorable bar was the Dark Horse, which used carousel horses as stools. The river ran directly under the wide floor planks, and we could hear the constant roaring below us.

Before the night officially ended, most everyone met up at the Dinner Belle, a restaurant that was open twenty-four hours, to order its specialty, Texas spaghetti (pasta with chili on top) served with Texas toast.

A year later, after the summer of 1969, instead of going back to Winona State College in Minnesota for our sophomore year, Patti and I decided to work in Aspen for the winter. In Aspen, I had a variety of jobs while attempting to be a ski bum. But I rarely strayed from the bunny slope.

In the evenings we often ended up at the J-Bar in the Hotel Jerome. I listened to stories about the old days when people just came to ski: they would stop by the bar for a drink or two, share their accounts of the slopes that day, check snow conditions for the next day, and be in bed by 7 p.m. I never saw John Denver, but I did get a glimpse of Elvis walking down the street. He was wearing sunglasses and a long fur coat, and looked shorter in person than onstage.

In the summer of 1970, I returned to Estes Park. The happening spot that year was the Black Canyon Inn, outside of Estes on Devil's Gulch Road. My roommate Peggy dated Frank, one of the managers, and we all received special treatment as friends of his girlfriend. One night we were surprised because someone was carding at the door. A cute guy asked for my ID and said, "This is a fake!" I replied: "Yes, it is, but I know Frank and he said it would be fine as long as we sat by the bar and only drank Coke." The fellow laughed and said "OK." Maybe he appreciated my honesty.

That's how I met Kent Whealy. Kent had graduated from the University of Kansas with a journalism degree in 1967 and planned to pursue a graduate degree in photography at Colorado State in Fort Collins. He and some friends had rented a cabin, and appeared in town in a bright yellow vintage MG TD convertible. Like so many others, Kent found Estes Park a fine spot for a working vacation.

We were both drawn to the beauty of the Rocky Mountains, and living in Estes Park was like being on a permanent vacation. Yet it was oddly unsatisfying. The mountains were majestic, splendid, consuming—but what can you do other than gaze at them? I felt distracted, and began to think about a more rooted, more meaningful life. I wanted a garden. I missed Mom's cold apple pie for breakfast. I thought life should be more.

Heading West

Kent and I began to travel, and realized how attracted we both were to food, beauty, and history. We briefly tried to live in his home state of Kansas, but as gardening became more important to us, we found the climate in Kansas challenging. We soon started dreaming of better gardens. British Columbia caught our attention, and we had also read of the fertile growing conditions in Oregon. In the late spring of 1971, we headed west.

Driving into western Oregon on Highway 101, we fell in love with Coos Bay and the Pacific Ocean. But lodging was scarce and expensive, and the inland climate was better for gardening. So after a few days, we reluctantly decided to spend our summer inland, in Elkton, a small town nestled in the Oregon coastal mountains, overlooking the emerald Umpqua River. The valley was dotted with small farms, and cows and sheep grazed the lush pastures. The gardens, orchards, and vineyards provided evidence of ample rainfall.

We stopped at a store on the town's only street, and a man there referred us to a group of small cabins on Bunches Bend that rented by the day or the week—an ideal place to stay while we searched for a house. It was an idyllic life. We picnicked in the Umpqua National Forest, always near a waterfall, on fresh melon and "kipper snacks," salted and smoked herring fillets that came in small tins like sardines, provided cheap protein, and needed no refrigeration. To pass the time, we drove by deserted homes in the river valley and explored abandoned fruit orchards.

Out for a drive one sunny Sunday afternoon, we noticed a large grove of older fruit trees in the middle of a pasture. We stopped at a nearby farmhouse and asked if we could pick some of the apples. The residents, an elderly couple, seemed pleased that we appreciated their orchard and told us to help ourselves. The day was so still that we could hear the apples snap as we plucked them from their branches. On one tree, every limb was loaded with perfect apples, orangish yellow with slight red stripes. We filled a big box to take back to the owners, who told us the variety was Gravenstein. "It's an old-timer," the farmer said. "My parents grew it. It's good for eating and makes the best applesauce and pies you can ever have." Gravenstein quickly became my favorite apple.

Another afternoon, we chanced upon a small stone house while driving down a back road. It was vacant, and in the back yard were blue and purple plum trees, heavy with ripe fruit. We sat on the hillside under the trees in the warmth of the September sun, eating sweet plums that had dropped to the ground. We could almost hear the conversations that once filled the rooms inside those broken walls, and we both began to dream of someday restoring that stone house and reliving the pioneer life in Oregon.

Despite the extended Colorado vacation, my life felt surprisingly grounded. I was becoming slightly suspicious that beneath my eagerness to be a carefree, adventurous woman, I might have some old-fashioned homemaker tendencies.

Eventually we found a cabin to rent, overlooking the river and close enough to hear its rushing water. The cabin was one large room

Gravenstein apple

with wooden floors and walls of rough unfinished lumber paneling. It was outfitted with an old black cast-iron cooking stove with pretty almond porcelain doors trimmed in nickel. There was no electricity and no indoor plumbing; we got our water from a hand pump and used an outhouse. The cabin was unfurnished except for a bed frame on stilts—actually just a piece of plywood that we could put our sleeping bags on.

Nearby, the river cascaded over huge boulders—perfect for steelhead trout and salmon. In the summer afternoons, we floated on the current from one boulder to the next. Then we would attempt to swim upstream, and always had great respect for the salmon afterwards.

Kent and I weren't concerned about money. He worked at the Oregon State Forestry tree farm about eight miles south of Elkton for minimum wage, which at that time was around $1.50 an hour. My waitressing experience from Colorado helped me land occasional work at the Freezet, a hamburger stand with soft-serve ice cream, owned by a local family. It was famous for the "secret salt" sprinkled on the French fries. I was on call when they were busy, at noon or after school when the kids came for treats. The wage was less than minimum and tips were nonexistent.

Most days I stayed at the cabin, or browsed the countryside for food. Wild blackberries grew everywhere, even right outside the door. I returned from walks with scratches, purple-stained fingers, and containers full of berries. We lived on blackberry muffins, blackberry pancakes topped with blackberries and blackberry syrup, blackberry cobbler, and blackberries with ice cream. I might have set a record for making the most blackberry jam and baking the most blackberry pies in Douglas County, Oregon.

I also canned many quarts of Gravenstein applesauce, cherries, blackberries, and plums. Canning on a wood stove was difficult—it took a lot of wood to maintain a constant boil in the canner for sterilizing jars and processing fruit.

The climate was mild, and as I picked and ate fresh plums, apricots, berries, cherries, and peaches, I felt that we'd found a Garden of Eden. But within a month of moving in, I found my Garden of Eden had other inhabitants. Some strange activities occurred in the kitchen overnight. One morning I found sticks on the kitchen cupboard beside my canning lids and jar rings. The lids and rings appeared to be messed up, and some of them were missing. Kent remembered he had heard a thumping sound during the night.

The next day I mentioned this strange incident to our neighbors, who identified the intruder as a pack rat. "Pack rats like shiny things. It probably dropped the sticks it had been taking to its nest and took a jar lid instead," one said. They also told me that the previous residents of the cabin had moved out because their child slept on the floor and they were nervous.

I took some comfort in knowing that pack rats were nocturnal plant-eaters and that our bed was on stilts, but I still felt unnerved. One day shortly afterwards, I went into the cabin and spotted the bushy varmint on the cupboard. Our eyes met, and we were both startled. With heart pounding, I ran out the door and he disappeared. Kent set a trap the next few nights, but the rat managed to trip it without getting caught.

Fortunately, we had become friends with Kent's supervisor from the tree farm and his wife. They owned a vacant restaurant, a former truck stop called the Roaring Camp Steakhouse, and offered to let us live there rent-free, if we would pay utilities. After we moved to the vacant truck stop, Kent thought it was amusing to pass by the kitchen in the morning and yell, "Order up, two eggs over easy, a short stack, and hold the toast."

Of course we had ladies' and men's restrooms, and each day we ate in a different booth. We slept on the floor in our sleeping bags. The kitchen had an industrial gas stove, commercial appliances, and running water—just what I needed to feed my canning addiction. We stored apples and everything else we could gather in the walk-in cooler.

Logging trucks made the highway noisy, but the back yard was beautiful. A gravel road curved toward a white wood-covered bridge, which led over Elk Creek and into the forest.

Elkton had fewer than two hundred residents and, like many small towns, felt wary of outsiders. It attracted a lot of them in the late '60s, mostly young West Coast urban refugees, "flower children" bent on self-sufficiency or just dropping out. Kent and I never felt we could be categorized as hippies—we were neither rebellious nor outrageous enough. And we didn't look the part: Kent had short hair, and I shaved my legs.

But we did believe in the virtue of living modestly off the land, and we did question the controlling social, economic, and political principles of our society, so in a sense we were anti-establishment. It's hard to say who took longer to warm to us—the locals or our fellow immigrants, like the group that ran the food co-op. There were rumors ("What if they're reporters doing an undercover story on hippies!") and suspicions ("Maybe they're narcs!"). But eventually the paranoia subsided.

We were particularly drawn to one couple, Charlie Cunningham and Valorie Brosig, who had moved to Elkton from California in late 1969 and were married in Drain, Oregon, on Christmas Eve. Charlie and Val were expecting their first child in September of 1970. Charlie worked with Kent at the tree farm and we all became good friends. We often met in town for coffee at Arlene's Café and General Store. The night their daughter was born, they stopped by our place on their way to the hospital in Drain to have a cup of tea and drop off their cat, Gooseberry.

Before winter, the Cunninghams moved back to California, but they didn't disappear from our lives. We would share more adventures together, far from Oregon. Kent and I, too, were concerned about what lay ahead if we stayed in Oregon. The next several months would be cool, foggy, and rainy, with little sunshine. The restaurant would be expensive to heat.

At the same time, we had news from Festina, and it was not good. Grandma Ott had had a stroke and Grandpa was not in the best of health. They still lived on the farm, but their children felt that they would be safer in a nursing home. Kent and I had both spent time with my grandparents and knew that leaving the farm would feel like the end of their lives. My grandparents' need for help, our dread of the long Oregon winter, and maybe our restless spirits made the decision to move back to Iowa a simple one.

In the course of relocating to Oregon from Kansas and Colorado, we had accumulated pets, including a full-grown St. Bernard named Ulara, a Persian cat with kittens, and boxes filled with enough canned goods to last many winters. We packed everything into our 1970 burnt orange VW Beetle, putting down the back seat to make room for a large pillow I'd sewn for Ulara. The car was packed solid; we had just enough room on the floor for the shift stick and our feet.

A blizzard hit the western edge of Wyoming as we were entering the state, closing the highway and stranding everyone. To make the story even livelier, a whole circus was snowed in with us, complete with elephants and the rest of the menagerie. Some people slept in the town jail cells. We found shelter in a church basement and slept on the floor with our dog and cats. Since we'd brought the boxes of canned goods into the church so they wouldn't freeze, Kent and I decided to bake a huge cherry cobbler for our new friends. And of course we all ate applesauce at every meal.

After two days, Interstate 80 reopened, but winds continued to drift snow over the highway. A young man who was stranded at the church needed a ride to Laramie and somehow managed to find a spot in the back seat. Whenever we got stuck, our passenger would hop out and give the Beetle a push.

My parents had worried about our trip back through snowy mountain passes and felt relieved when we arrived in Iowa, even with our own menagerie and somewhat unconventional appearance. (My mother pushed one of the old guilt buttons, scolding me to "Put on a bra!")

Gardening in Iowa

We'd moved back to rescue my grandparents from a nursing home, but the family had come up with a plan that allowed Grandma and Grandpa to stay on their farm. Still, here we were, and it seemed as good a time and place as any to settle down.

In November Kent and I were married in Our Lady of Seven

Dolors Catholic Church in Festina. Father Graff, who was to perform the ceremony, commented that this would be the first "mixed marriage" he had ever performed. We were surprised to learn he was referring to Kent's not being Catholic. To please my parents, we wanted to be married in the church, and for that to happen the priest had to give us a special dispensation.

"Why are you marrying this man?" Father Graff asked.

"Because I love him?"

"That is not on the list of accepted answers."

I was surprised. "What are my choices?"

"Are you pregnant?"

"No."

"Was there a lack of Catholic men to choose from in the community?"

I knew that would never work.

The final choice was, "Are you trying to convert him to Catholicism?"

That sounded good. We paid $50 for the dispensation and Father Graff sent the request to the archdiocese in Dubuque.

The wedding was a traditional Catholic affair, the church ceremony at 11 o'clock, followed by a reception at the Knights of Columbus Hall in Ossian. At noon, there was a home-cooked dinner prepared by my parents' neighbors. That part of Iowa has a wedding tradition in which the bride is taken, usually against her will, to all the taverns in the neighboring small towns. If a bride comes into a tavern, the owner is obligated to serve free drinks to everyone. My cousin was driving the wedding car, and I hoped that he would forget the tradition. He didn't, but eventually I made it to my own wedding reception.

We spent the rest of the afternoon drinking kegs of Schmidt beer, visiting, and dancing. Kent's parents and grandparents came from Kansas, and with his brother there were five people attending from his family. The pews on my side of the church had been filled with more than one hundred aunts, uncles, cousins, and neighbors.

By 5 o'clock most everyone had left the party; my uncles all had to get home to milk. Kent and I took a box with two dinners and wedding cake to Grandpa and Grandma Ott. I was still wearing my wedding dress and Kent was in his suit. We sat in their living room and retold the story of our wedding day. Grandpa Ott got up from the couch, took my veil off, and tenderly placed the layers of white lace on Grandma's head. They started to dance and soon we were all dancing in their living room. In the kitchen as we were leaving, Grandpa said, "Seien Sie zu einander gut": "Be good to each other."

Kent and I looked forward to finding a farmhouse in northeast Iowa. After fantasizing about living in abandoned farm sites in Oregon, we were now living our dream. Fortunately, the farmhouse we rented had not been abandoned; it was in excellent condition: wooden floors, vintage wallpaper, beautiful oak woodwork, built-in cupboards, china cabinets with leaded glass. The kitchen had pine wainscoting and a large solid oak door that opened into a superb pantry lined with empty shelves. The basement was clean and cool, with a root cellar and plenty of space to store canned goods. There was running water and a drain for my Speed Queen wringer washing machine. Just outside the cellar door was the clothesline. A large porch wrapped around the south and east sides of the house.

During that first winter in Iowa, we spent many afternoons at

Grandpa Ott's farm, and I learned what a powerful storyteller he had become. Grandpa had never been out of the state and very few times out of Fayette County, yet his life was full and he was content. Maybe I was just listening more closely, knowing he was ill.

In the spring, I would finally have my first garden. It felt like a very adult thing to do. My grandparents, uncles, and aunts could visit us and look at our garden just as I'd looked at theirs. We'd have purple morning glories growing on the east porch and train them on twine just as Grandpa did, leaving a spot open to watch the cars go by. We might even sit out on the porch and actually recognize the drivers.

Morning glory, after an engraving by E. Sears

One cold February afternoon when we were visiting, Kent asked Grandpa for some of the morning glory seeds. He gave us a few of the tiny black seeds in a white cardboard pillbox and mentioned that the morning glories came to St. Lucas when my great-grandparents emigrated from Bavaria. I could feel my imagination simmering, and soon I could see my distant relatives in Germany. They were waking up as these same purple morning glories opened to the sun. The men might be leaving to go out to the fields, or perhaps it was Sunday and everyone was sitting on the porch telling stories or watching the children play. Now we would become part of that family tradition. We would keep the seed and the story of Grandpa Ott's morning glory alive.

The next summer, Kent and I were sitting on the front porch. I was eight months pregnant with our first child and relishing the warm quiet afternoon. A car drove in, made a slow turn around the circle drive, and stopped in front. Grandpa Ott was out by himself on a rare Sunday drive in his robin's-egg blue 1962 Chevrolet Biscayne. Grandpa never got out of the car. He just rolled down his car window and chatted with us about the weather and the upcoming baby. He noticed the morning glories, said that I should have thinned them more, and smiled.

We'd spent our first winter in Iowa dreaming of gardens. My parents and Kent's mother always ordered their seed from Gurney's Seed and Nursery Company in Yankton, South Dakota. We didn't know how many more seed catalogs there might be out there. Our garden spot was big—actually the size of a baseball field, because it *was* a baseball field, complete with a wire backstop. We ordered one packet of everything. Huber's Store in Fort Atkinson carried seed potatoes and onions, and my parents gave us kohlrabi and German Pink tomato plants. Grandma Ott knew that I loved her deep pink dahlias and gave me a few bulbs to plant by the garage. The dahlia patch became a frustration, though, because our goat, Jake, ate the buds just as they were about to bloom.

I gathered canning recipes and jars from my mother, Kent's mother, all the grandparents, aunts, and neighbors. I was constantly sterilizing jars, by boiling them for thirty minutes, draining them on the kitchen counter, and covering them with a clean cotton dish towel while they waited to be filled. Each evening I would go to bed with a stack of recipes, the local church cookbooks, and a Ball canning book to plan for the next day. I would go off to sleep comforted by the sound of jar lids popping as they sealed, one by one.

Most memorable that summer were the beautiful celery, onions, and bushels of German Pink tomatoes. I canned delicious soup and bottled tomato juice and catsup. (My mom's catsup recipe called for a spice bag: "Take a small white square of cotton cloth, fill the middle with cloves, allspice, and cinnamon sticks, and tie shut with string; add the tomato juice and cook till thick, or about 3 hours." The house would smell wonderful for days!) My mother would never use a water bath to can juice or catsup—only sterile bottles and new caps. I bought new glass bottles and gold metal bottle caps and borrowed my parents' bottle capper. While we had the bottle capper we also decided to make homemade root beer with Hires extract.

The Empress green beans were another favorite. I canned many quarts of beans without a pressure canner, so to be sure that harmful organisms were eliminated, the beans had to simmer in a water bath for three hours. I made sauerkraut in a crock, made lime pickles, searched for wild plums and elderberries for jelly, dug horseradish to grate—basically I canned or pickled everything.

In addition to having a large garden, we amassed a collection of poultry. It started with just a few laying hens, Brown Leghorns and then bigger Buff Orpingtons. I grew up with Bantams and appreciated their iridescent emerald green and blue feathers and their chicks, which looked like baby pheasants. A farmer near St. Lucas gave us a few. We met a woman who lived between Waucoma and Alpha, and from her farm we added two Embden geese named Gordie and Gertie. Several Pearl Guineas became our watch hens—their distinctive calls sounded something like "buckwheat!" We had Khaki Campbell runner ducks, mallards, and Muscovies, which are capable of hatching broods of more than twenty ducklings at one setting. Turkeys soon followed.

A child's plastic swimming pool was buried in the chicken yard so the ducks and geese could swim. We gathered eggs constantly, not only from the chicken coop but also from anywhere the guineas laid their eggs in the chicken yard. A neighbor had an incubator, and would hatch chicks, goslings, ducklings, and even little keets (baby guineas) to add to our flock.

Pea pods, after a photograph by Charles Jones

On the Road Again

❧

We stayed in Iowa for over a year, and we loved it. But there was no money coming in, and Kent had a job waiting for him back in Wellington, Kansas, where his parents, Bud and Edna, had spent most of their lives. Edna's parents, Lloyd and Murrel Coffelt, who were always called Dada and Nana, lived across the alley. We liked the idea of being close to our other family, and the winter in Kansas would certainly be milder. Plus, I think we both felt the desire to keep on exploring.

Our son, Aaron, had been born in September 1972. The plan was for me and the baby to fly Frontier Airlines from Waterloo to Wichita, where we'd meet Kent. He would drive a rented U-Haul truck and tow our VW Beetle. Even with the truck we were forced to leave some things behind—like the wringer washer I'd bonded with. But we packed pretty much everything else, except the goat. We had our flock of Buff Orpingtons in cages surrounded with boxes of canning and furniture. On the drive down to Kansas, Kent said, when he stopped for gas, everyone at the truck stop was entertained by the rooster crows coming from the back of the truck.

His parents had found a light green ranch home for us to rent, on a farm about five miles from Wellington on the Botkin Road. It was smaller than our Iowa house, but big enough for the three of us. There was a horse barn, but no chicken coop. Luckily we found a neighbor who was happy to have our Buff Orpingtons. We would drive by every morning on the way into town to feed the chickens and pick up the eggs.

Also along the Botkin Road was the H. L. Stewart Greenhouse. When I passed their trash cans, I would notice piles of flowers and could not resist stopping to rescue a bouquet now and then. One day I was caught with a handful of daffodils and felt sheepish. The young man, Kurt Baucum, whose parents owned the greenhouse, assured me he didn't mind a bit. Kurt said, "Come inside. If you like these spent flowers you will really enjoy this." I stepped into the greenhouse and was overpowered by the scent of gardenias. "My grandfather planted this gardenia bush directly into the ground in the greenhouse over forty years ago," Kurt told me. "Gardenias are very fragile and bruise so easily they could not be shipped quickly enough for weddings. I remember one of my jobs as a kid was to pick the fresh blossoms." Kurt was a delight, brought gardenias to our house often, and became one of our best friends in Wellington.

In Kansas, Kent and I continued to garden and dream. We played yahoo and pitch with Nana and Dada. Nana gave me her farm pickle recipe and told stories about living in a sod house in Oklahoma. Dada told stories about being in World War I and a shoot-out in Dalton, Kansas. Kent's mother was also a canning-aholic so we were constantly canning or freezing—peaches, tomatoes, whatever the garden yielded. She made the best peach ice cream. Kent's father was calm and more than willing to assist the rest of the family in our excesses.

We watched three crops of wheat being harvested. We sought out every orchard in the county and picked sour cherries, apricots, peaches, and pecans. I learned to appreciate okra fried in cornmeal, creamed new peas and potatoes in June, and fresh sweet potatoes and turnips in September. Many local gardeners were happy to share their growing tips, tomatoes, and seeds. I sold Super Sioux tomatoes to a few families. And I learned the frustrations of sun-scald on the tomatoes, and daily temperatures over 100 degrees. On hot afternoons, we drove to Oxford, where the Arkansas River powered a water mill. There, we cooled off in the river and bought seven-grain cereal sewn in a cloth bag.

Eventually we moved into a three-story white farmhouse in the middle of wheat fields, buffeted by prairie

Yugoslavian Finger
Fruit and gourds

winds that blew fine red soil into the house. I encountered chiggers there, after sitting in the grass beside the row of peas I was picking, and found a black snake in the basement. We had a chicken coop, and rescued a three-legged dog named Hobble. We transplanted redbud trees from the woods and trumpet vine that had grown near the out-house at Kent's grandparents' farm. Grandpa Ott's morning glories adapted well to southern Kansas.

Kent worked for the Wellington street department and then for Boeing Aircraft in Wichita. Wherever we went, we seemed to attract an eclectic group of friends. In Kansas, the most memorable was a former star of Hollywood B movies who drove a Volkswagen van and persuaded us (briefly) to be vegetarians and practice Kundalini yoga. We never did wear turbans, though.

The Whealys' three-story farmhouse near Wellington, Kansas

Kansas Peaches

Kansas was very hot in the summer. But there was a bonus—that's when the peaches ripened.

All winter and spring I'd been fantasizing about the family-owned peach orchards around Wichita and Wellington. I asked Nana what her favorite peach was. "I love Redhaven," she said. "They're early and you'll never find a peach so sweet and juicy, but the skins are fragile, so you pick them a little greener to take home. The Bellaires are usually next and then Glohavens, which can be the size of a softball. The last to ripen are the Cresthavens and Redskins, and they're the best for canning. Just to eat from the tree, the best is Belle of Georgia—such juicy white flesh!"

On a late July afternoon, when the sun was not so strong and the winds had died down, Nana invited us to go with her and Dada to their favorite peach orchard in Belle Plaine, operated by the Belle family since the late 1800s. (The town itself was named for Belle Plaine, Iowa, hometown of one of its early settlers.)

"I think the Redhaven peaches should be ready, and the Belles will have White Hale peaches too," Nana said. "Not many orchards still have those."

Kent and I and our year-old son piled into their 1959 Chevrolet. We put half-peck and bushel baskets and sheet cake pans and cardboard flats in the trunk, and headed for Belle Plaine on Sumner County's sandy roads. The car had no air conditioning, and dust blew in the open windows from plowed fields awaiting seeding to milo or soybeans.

We drove up to the farm stand and told the owners we were there to pick peaches. Nana said to Mr. Belle, "How long have you had this orchard?"

"My grandfather found this quarter-section of land in the spring of 1873," Mr. Belle told us. "He knew the soil was fertile and it was enclosed by good hedge fencing. He planted 1,000 peach trees, 165 cherry trees, and 500 apple trees."

Nana told him she had been coming to this orchard every summer for as long as she could remember. "Where should we pick today?" she asked. Mr. Belle said, "Go to the north end of the orchard, that's where the ripest peaches are. You'll find ladders out there—just stop back here on your way out."

The trees were heavy with ripe fruit. I climbed up the ladder with a bucket and as I reached out to pick a peach, it fell into my hand. I felt I had to eat this perfect fruit right there on the ladder. "Mmmmmm," I said, peach juice dripping from my chin and elbows. "This is the best peach I have ever eaten."

"They'll have to weigh you, too, when we're done picking," Dada replied. Mr. Belle had said to eat all we could hold.

Nana was very particular about stacking the peaches in the bushel basket. "Place the peaches in full circles, one on top of the other," she said. "That way you get the most peaches in the basket."

We filled our baskets, loaded them into the trunk, and drove back to the farm stand. Mr. Belle was waiting for us and we paid him by the bushel, then used a hand water pump to wash the peach juice and dust from our sticky arms, hands, and faces. To prevent the fruit on the bottom of the bushel from being squished, Nana took most of the peaches from the baskets and laid them out in the trays and empty flats.

Once we got home, we sorted the peaches according to ripeness.

Those that could wait a day or so for canning were kept on picnic tables outside in the shade. The bruised peaches would be made into peach butter. The ripest ones were canned that evening. Putting the peaches up while they were still warm from the summer sun was the best of canning—no other jar of peaches would have such a golden glow.

A Reunion

We had kept in touch with our friends Val and Charlie Cunningham from Oregon, and learned that they felt dissatisfied with where they were living. One evening, Charlie called us. "We still have the home-steading bug," he said, "but land in California is crazy expensive. Everyone wants to move west to garden in warm weather."

"Not many folks are flocking to the Midwest—the winters are too cold," Kent replied. "You and Val should just pack up your stuff and move back here. We can buy land together." Not long afterwards, Charlie and Val arrived, with two young daughters and little else, to live with us in Kansas. All native Californians, none of them had ever experienced a true Midwest thunderstorm. One hot summer evening, they got their *Wizard of Oz* moment.

It was a typical July day, the temperature peaking at over 100 degrees, with a strong wind coming from the south—the wind blows almost nonstop in that corner of Kansas, from sunup to sundown. Kent's mother had called earlier to tell us Sumner County was under a tornado warning till 9, but what else was new? Kent and I went outside to cool off after supper. We could hear distant rumblings of thunder, and the western sky was dark purple, almost black, with wispy gray billows moving low in the sky. The air was filled with an eerie yellow haze.

The hot winds finally stopped for the first time all day, and a sense of calm set in. But as quickly as the south wind died down, the west wind picked up. Our faces were stinging as a gust threw fine sand at us from the driveway. We ran inside to close the windows, the rain pelting us through screens already plastered with leaves.

Charlie and Val were upstairs getting the girls ready for bed. A streak of lightning lit the sky, followed by a peal of thunder loud enough to rattle the glass in the windows. The next thing we heard was Charlie and Val coming down the stairs, each carrying a frightened daughter wrapped in a blanket. Just as they entered the living room, a tremendous bolt of lightning sent tentacles across the sky as far as we could see. One tentacle struck the power pole next to the house, sounding like a cannon shot, followed by shock waves that we could actually feel. The electricity was knocked out.

We found matches to light candles and Nana's kerosene lantern, and sat together in the living room for the next half-hour while the lightning cracked and danced around us and thunder boomed. Charlie said he felt as if a sizzling net was being cast over our house. In the fleeting illumination of lightning, we saw sheets of rain, punctuated with branches and leaves. The weeping willow was almost touching the ground; the wind ripped branches from other trees and threw them into the yard. Then hail the size of golf balls started pounding at the windows and bouncing off the ground, sending up wisps of steam from soil still hot from the blazing sun.

Aaron, who was three, ran from window to window, excited by the storm. Our baby, Amy, in my arms, seemed undisturbed. But Charlie and Val's girls were crying, and maybe their parents were as well.

"Do you think we should go down into the basement?" Val asked.

Earlier in the summer I'd seen a large black snake slithering through the dog's door into the basement. It wasn't a place I wanted to be with no more illumination than a kerosene lamp. "Oh, it's not that bad," I said. "Let's not go down yet."

Finally, there was a silence. I started to open windows, to let fresh breezes cool down the house.

"Gee, was that some strange initiation to the Midwest?" Charlie asked later.

Kent and I both thought, "Just wait for the blizzards!"

Missouri Bound

Kent and I had already begun thinking about northern Missouri as a place to look for land. Whenever we visited my parents, we traveled north on Interstate 35 and the rolling hills around Bethany always caught our eye. We'd often picnic with Aaron and Amy along the Grand River, halfway between my family in Iowa and Kent's family in Kansas. This part of Missouri was quite isolated, and we knew the land prices would be reasonable and the taxes low.

Soon after the Cunninghams came to live with us, Kent and Charlie took off on a scouting trip to northern Missouri, leaving Val, me, and the kids in Kansas. The guys explored Gilmore, Milan, Unionville, Cainsville, and every other small town in the area. They tore out the yellow pages from local phone books containing the names and addresses of real estate agents and newspapers. When they returned to Kansas, we put together our wish list for the homestead: rural, but close to a small town, about sixty acres, mostly wooded, with some clearings for gardens and orchards. Charlie and Val wanted a farmhouse; Kent and I had dreams of building our own home. We addressed about two hundred envelopes, stuffed our Land Wanted letter inside, and hoped for the best.

Within a month we had received many calls and letters. The most promising was from Joe Dale Linn, who phoned us from Missouri after reading our ad in the *Princeton Post-Telegraph*. "I've got just the property you're looking for," he said. "About eighty acres, nice woods, some cleared land, a smaller farmhouse, and a point on a ridge overlooking the Weldon River valley that would be a great building site."

It was time for Charlie, Val, and their daughters to check things out. They looked at abandoned farms, houses without roofs, land with no roads, and land close to a town with a business district that consisted of a tavern. They decided to leave Joe Dale Linn's property for last. When they did check it out, Charlie called. "You would not believe how perfect this land is. There's a small house enclosed with an oak woods and farther down the road a fantastic view of the valley. Princeton is a nice town, and the countryside is beautiful. We drove on a ridge road into town with views of rolling hills for miles and miles."

As soon as we could, we all went back to Princeton and met with Mr. Linn. There was no question about it: this was the place. On July 25, 1975, Charlie and Val bought thirty acres with the house, Kent and I bought thirty acres with the building site, and we bought twenty acres of bottomland in common.

In the rural style, the farm was known by the name of the last farmers to have owned it. This one was the Ada Holt place. Ada and her husband, Dorald, lived there until he died in 1968. After his death, Ada went to live with her daughter; Joe Dale Linn and his wife, Mary Castell, eventually bought the property. Joe was a speculator who had bought the Holt place along with several other farms in the area. He'd planned to build a dam that would flood the whole valley below, and then sell house sites on the resulting lake. But he gave up on his scheme and was ready to move on.

The end of his dream was the beginning of ours. We bought the property for less than $10,000. Charlie and Val moved up before winter and we moved in the late spring of 1976.

The Big Move

Before leaving for Missouri, we put an ad in the *Wellington Daily News* to sell our little orange Beetle. I felt a bit sad as the new owner drove it down the street, so carefree. We then bought a blue 1962 Chevy short-bed truck with a wooden camper that fit over the truck bed, and Kent went ahead to find a place for us to rent. A few days later, he called to say he'd met a young couple, Garry and Judy Cox, who farmed about three miles from our land; Garry's great-aunt, Hazel Derry, had passed away and her house was empty.

"He said we could live there rent-free while we build our house," Kent said. "They have kids almost the ages of Amy and Aaron and are excited to have a young couple move into the neighborhood. The house looks nice—lots of bedrooms. Garry said it was actually two houses moved together. There's a rhubarb bed, patches of lily of the valley, lots of hostas, live-forever, yucca, and purple phlox blooming around a root cellar. I can't wait for you to see it!"

The pioneers, no doubt, faced a considerable challenge in packing their Conestoga wagons for westward trips over the Santa Fe trails. But packing for a modern-day homesteading adventure was no picnic either. We had the *Whole Earth Catalog*: a Gravely tractor, a Franklin woodstove, a Corona grain mill, many tools, a Blue Ball canning book, and lots of canning jars. When we tied the rocking chair to the top of the truck, I felt like the Clampetts.

The house was five and a half hours away, about thirteen miles northeast of Princeton. We drove up and down the hills on Route P, a paved road, and then followed about three miles of narrow gravel

Scarlet Nantes carrots

38

roads. As the road was winding down a steep hill, Kent said, "There on the left side is Garry's Great-Aunt Hazel's house." Garry and Judy were waiting for us there.

The house had gray shingle siding, with white curtains softly moving in open windows. It was a warm summer day, but the fresh breezes made the house feel cool. There were four bedrooms, a spacious living room, a nice kitchen, and a screened-in porch. The bathroom had a large tub and light pink fixtures. I was so happy to know we had a comfortable place to stay while we were building our house (at one point we had considered living in a teepee). As we were discussing heating and water, Garry offered to show us the cistern.

My parents' farm had a cistern that collected rainwater from the house roof. Mom used the water for washing clothes; we had a well for drinking water. Most of the cisterns in Iowa were built of stone and had long since been filled in. Hardly anyone used cisterns anymore.

In the back yard was a small gray storage shed, wood-sided. The double wooden doors on the ground alongside it opened to stone steps going down to the root cellar, Garry said, though he called it "the cave." "That's where my Great-Aunt Hazel stored her canning and potatoes.

"Right here by this old cast-iron hand pump is the cistern," he added. "It's just covered up with this board. Be sure to keep the lid on tight so no one falls in and drowns. You can find a big rock for the top, which helps." When his great-aunt lived there, Garry said, he had to come over and check the cistern because the water tasted off: "I opened the wooden door over the top and found a dead squirrel that had somehow fallen in and drowned."

We lived in Missouri for eight years—two years at Garry's Great-Aunt Hazel's house and six at our own. Never once did I drink water from the cistern. Instead, I saved empty milk jugs and filled them at the Princeton laundromat. In the summer, I filled a large cooler at the Princeton City Park.

The Early Years in Missouri

Kent and I intended to build our house with lumber harvested from the land, feed ourselves from the gardens and orchards, and someday make a living selling strawberries and saving and selling seed. We already had a small collection.

I planted a large patch of Senator Dunlap strawberries, asparagus, rhubarb, horseradish, and other homesteading staples on our new ground. We planted fifty-seven fruit trees on a north-facing slope beside the road to the river bottom. They were mostly apple trees, but we were eager to have Red Haven peaches, so we added peach and cherry trees. That first summer we lost about sixteen trees because of a drought, but we weren't discouraged. (Some of the apple trees remain, and the people who now live at our former house have a cherry-picking ritual each year. They pick enough for only one pie, but it's a good one!)

Watching the sun rise and set from our hilltop was spectacular. Unfortunately, so were the north winds. We quickly planted a windbreak of white and jack pine and autumn olive. The road was graded and graveled, ending with a circle drive in front of our imaginary house on the point. We cut walnut, white oak, and hickory from the woods and sent them to the local sawmill to dry.

Bob, from the Princeton State Bank, was very friendly, but the bank had never lent money for a house built with telephone poles, and he didn't intend to start with us. Building without a construction loan meant hands-on work by our family, some of whom no doubt remember every board and stone. The house was like a puzzle. Amy would often tag along with me to search through the pile of rocks outside for one with the perfect shape. Aaron was eager to carry it back to what would eventually become the fireplace.

The power company erected poles to bring electricity to the house site. By fall, with an electric skillet and a water jug, I could cook a meal at our new "house." We felt that we'd made a respectable start before winter.

Looking back, I realize that it's sometimes a blessing to be a bit ignorant of the challenges ahead. Had I known, I might have seriously rethought this homesteading adventure.

Fortunately, we had Garry's Great-Aunt Hazel's house to settle into. I was in the routine of going to the laundromat in Princeton, and started to look forward to laundry day. (I should have recognized the early warning signs of homesteaders' burnout.) I would get out of the house, buy groceries, and maybe the kids and I would get ice cream. To save money, I tried not to use the coin-operated dryers; when it was warm enough, I loved hanging clothes on the line to dry after I got home, and in the evening the sheets made the bedrooms smell like fresh air.

Hyacinth bean and hummingbird

In the winter, life was harder. Sometimes we waited days for the snowplows to clear the roads. We stacked straw and hay bales around the foundation to keep the floors warmer, and with any luck to keep the water pipes from freezing. But the pipes still froze, and we lived in fear that when they thawed, we would have to shut the water off. When we didn't have water, we melted snow or used a hand pump to get water from the barn cistern. One winter night Kent returned to the house with an empty bucket and the pump handle in his hand. It was so cold the handle just broke. Soon my life centered on frozen water pipes, snowed-in roads, and mice that found our home a better option than the outdoors.

The True Seed Exchange

*The greatest service which can be rendered any
country is to add a useful plant to its culture.*

THOMAS JEFFERSON

Not long after my grandfather entrusted Kent and me with his morning glory and tomato seeds, we realized how precious they had become. After Grandpa Ott died in 1974, we were the only family members with his seed. Around that time we were reading articles that described the dangers of losing genetic diversity. We began to see

that the introduction of commercial farming had severely diminished the diversity found in food crops.

Kent and I had a handful of seeds, a story, and a warning. We started to speculate about other gardeners who were keeping seed brought to this country when their families immigrated. We knew that seeds used for favorite foods back home—reminders of the old country—were hidden away in personal belongings like apron pockets and ferried across the ocean. Those same seeds were then grown on American soil where, over time, they became acclimated to local conditions, and were passed down through generations in families.

I remembered my grandmothers trading and sharing seed and "starts" with relatives or neighbors. They often left someone's house with an envelope of seeds or a water-soaked handkerchief rolled around a "slip" from a houseplant. Their kitchen windowsills were lined with glass jars filled with water; delicate white root hairs sprouted from an African violet leaf or a begonia cutting.

In 1974, when we were still in Kansas, Kent had written letters to various back-to-the-land magazines—*Countryside*, *Mother Earth News*, *Landward Ho*—in an attempt to discover others who were saving heirloom seed. Responses arrived from five or six of them. Like propagating seeds, the word began to spread.

Our modest dream of saving seed with like-minded people became a reality in 1975. Twenty-nine gardeners from all over the United States and Canada sent 25 cents and a large envelope to the True Seed Exchange; in return, they received a six-page publication listing seed that other gardeners were willing to share. It seemed like a low initial response, but Kent and I were willing to be patient. The correspondence that first year was so enjoyable that the yearbook included all the members' letters in their entirety. Their personal stories gave life to the seeds they offered—that first tiny publication is a treasure.

By the next year, our group had grown to 142 members from forty states, Canada, Guatemala, and Ecuador. We had no idea how many other gardeners were still keeping old varieties, but we were on our way.

The 1976 *True Seed Exchange* was printed on a hand-cranked mimeograph machine set up in the back bedroom of Great-Aunt Hazel's house. (Kent and I later donated this machine to Our Lady of Seven Dolors in Festina to be used for weekly church bulletins.)

It was a no-frills publication, printed on white 8½ × 11 paper, but its beauty was in the carefully written variety descriptions. Kent and I assembled the seventeen-page booklet, stapled the top corner, and folded it in half. After hand-addressing, it was ready for mailing, third class, at the Princeton Post Office. We charged $1 per subscription but it wasn't quite enough to cover our expenses, and we had a shortfall of $35.

In 1978, Kent was working in Lamoni as a cameraman at Printcraft, whose owner, Jack Buntin, was interested in the Exchange. After looking at copies of the first two publications, Jack said we needed a cover picture. The cover of the third *True Seed Exchange* has a picture of five-year-old Aaron, sitting on a pile of boards in front of our house and holding one of the largest German Pink tomatoes of the season.

Because the publication had grown, we decided to take advantage of the printing press. We used cover stock, and the pages were stapled in the middle and opened like a book. This third publication was thirty-two pages and went to three hundred members; we didn't have space to print all their letters. The organization lost some quirks as it grew, but extra members strengthened the Exchange through their knowledge and their spirit of teamwork.

The *1976–77 True Seed Exchange* listed Johnny's Selected Seeds as "a source of good seed." In the 1978 edition, we included two pages of commercial seed sources and named nineteen catalogs that were rich with heirloom seed and useful information. Of the catalogs listed in 1978, less than half remain today: Johnny's Selected Seeds, the Redwood City Seed Company, Le Jardin du Gourmet, Vermont Bean Seed Company, Southmeadow Fruit Gardens, and J. L. Hudson, Seedsman.

The "Seed Saving Guide" was attached to and an integral part of the *1976–77 True Seed Exchange*. As caretakers of my grandfather's seeds, Kent and I were always aware of the importance of keeping the seed pure. Gardeners needed to know how to grow seed correctly to avoid cross-pollination, and how to cure and store the saved seed. And then there's the most obvious yet critical piece of seed-saving advice: Never plant all of your seed.

The *1976–77 True Seed Exchange* also included a "Companion

Planting Guide," which listed plants that benefit from growing near each other. In 1978 we added a section called "Hodgepodge," my favorite, a miscellany of intriguing gardeners' tips and comments from readers. Mrs. Wayne Dorrough from Sullivan, Missouri, wrote: "Castor beans and Scilia bulbs planted in the garden will keep moles out." Robert Fitzgerald contributed another gem: "After planting cabbage, cut some stalks of rhubarb and stick a piece down in the soil between each plant. No pests will bother your cabbage."

The garden writer Nancy Bubel, who died in 2009, wrote to let us know she was including a chapter on our organization in her forthcoming book from Rodale Press, *The New Seed-Starters Handbook*—encouraging news! But as the weather turned cold in 1978, finances were tight and it was time to compile the fourth *True Seed Exchange*. We had hoped to move into the basement of our homestead before winter, but we rescheduled for spring. You can never trust contractors to keep on schedule—even if the contractors are yourselves.

Changes

For four years, we called ourselves the True Seed Exchange, to stress that we were trying to save heirloom seeds that produced true to type each year—nonhybrids, in other words. In 1979, Kent and I decided to change the name to Seed Savers Exchange.

We were all seed savers, literally saving old seed from being lost. Many once-imperiled varieties were now offered by more than one member. Heirloom seed was circulating between members and through the Seed Savers Exchange. And SSE was growing into more than an exchange: it was becoming a repository as well—a seed bank that included both the Whealy collection and the seeds of other gardeners.

The first cover image by
Judith Ann Griffith

The first *True Seed Exchange* newsletter printed a note from Lina
Sisco of Winona, Missouri, one of the original listed members:

> I have been gardening for more years than I like to think about
> and I do love to raise all kinds of stuff and do lots of canning. I
> share with lots of people from my garden. So I am sending you
> two kinds of beans that I raise. The Bird Egg beans have been
> in my family for many, many years as my grandmother brought
> them to Missouri some time in the 1880s. As for Paul Bunyan
> beans, I got the seed from Oregon, but understand they are a
> very old bean. So they are all free to you. Hope you have good
> luck with them. I am sending my quarter and envelope.

Lina passed away two years later, but her Bird Egg bean was offered in the *1979 Seed Savers Exchange*, by our son Aaron and others. Here was evidence that the vision of collecting, saving, and distributing heirloom seed had actually achieved what Kent and I had hoped for. SSE was able to save a seed from extinction.

Fifteen years after the first newsletter, Becky Silva of Vancouver, Washington, sent a note published in *Seed Savers 1990 Summer Edition*:

Lina Sisco, one of the first members of the 1975 True Seed Exchange

I was going through some old *Mother Earth News* magazines that were given to me and was reading your interview in the 1982 January/February issue which I found very interesting. I had been thinking of some special beans my grandma used to have. Then you mentioned Lina Sisco and her Bird Egg beans. Lina was my grandma! Lina was proud of those beans, which she had been given by her grandmother, who brought them to Missouri in the 1880s. One year Lina sent us some when I was little. I remember being in awe of "Granny's Beans."

Well, it seems my mom can't find those beans and I doubt they were ever planted because my folks aren't garden-ers. I've been gardening for three years but after reading your article am quite interested in "heirloom" varieties. And I would like to start with Granny's Bird Egg bean. Can you put me in touch with someone who'd be willing to share a few? I loved Grandma Lina. She called herself the "fat squaw," and it would mean so much to me to grow her beans.

Lina Sisco's Bird Egg beans

SSE sent Becky some of the beans, now identified as Lina Sisco's Bird Egg bean. It's a popular bean for planting, and we also sell it as dried eating beans. I love stories with happy endings.

The Missouri Visitor

In the late 1970s, Kent read about a fellow in Arizona who was doing interesting work and began corresponding with him. Gary Paul Nabhan, a graduate student, was making trips into the remote mountains of Mexico and collecting seeds from villages. He would then distribute them to Native Americans whose tribes had lost the seed for those crops. Gary was a talented writer, and in 1976 succeeded in getting an article published in *Organic Gardening* magazine.

Gary and Kent continued corresponding, and in the summer of 1980, Gary bought a bus ticket from Arizona to Bethany, Missouri. Our third child, Tracy, was then only a few months old, and our homestead wasn't completed—we had minimal plumbing, plastic covering the windows, and unfinished floors. Gary was to be our first overnight guest. I was happy for the company, but a little concerned that having a visitor would keep us from completing work on the house before winter.

The bowling alley in Bethany, about thirty-five miles from our house, served as the bus station. Kent took off in our truck to pick Gary up, and I fell asleep before they returned. That was just as well, because it would have been a long wait. They bought a six-pack of beer and stopped at Lake Paho, about four miles west of Princeton. Kent told me later that he and Gary had sat on the shore and talked for hours about what was important in their lives, about their dreams and hopes for saving seeds.

Gary was a delightful guest. We soon got used to his quick-witted sense of humor, and we all hit it off. We spent many afternoons sitting on the deck, taking turns holding our baby daughter, while watching as Aaron rode his bike and Amy rode her tricycle around the driveway; our dog, Pokey, ran back and forth between them.

Discussions among the adults ranged widely. Gary had been a prime mover in starting Southwest Traditional Crop Conservancy Garden and Seed Bank in Tucson and was beginning to explore the possibilities of forming a nonprofit organization devoted to Native American plants. Kent and I knew there were plenty of seeds to be saved, and not enough time. The prospect of another seed-saving organization, focusing on particular crops, excited us. And we were eager to learn about fund-raising. Gary remembers Kent asking, "Just how do you write a grant?"

Full Time in Missouri

One SSE member, John Hartman, now deceased, told us, "You've got a tiger by the tail." And Seed Savers Exchange definitely had momentum of its own. We had a tiger by the tail—now what? We knew the organization had not even begun to reach its growth potential, and wouldn't unless we poured our energy into the cause. But how would we support ourselves while SSE grew?

The publicity that Seed Savers Exchange had received was more than we'd hoped for. SSE had already been recognized in more than one hundred magazines and other media. The interest was at times overwhelming, but the enthusiasm was heartening. A front-page story in the *Los Angeles Times* on June 2, 1980, summed up the situation and drew a lot of attention to John Withee, a noted collector of bean seeds from Maine, as well as to Kent and SSE:

> As these heirlooms are ceremoniously mailed around the country each winter, planted each spring, and then harvested in the fall for the next year's mailing, seed savers provide an important genetic "fail-safe"—a chain of small backup seed repositories for the big government center in Fort Collins, Colorado, where thousands of varieties are supposed to be saved for posterity. The backup is especially important because government repositories are so low on funds they cannot always do what they are supposed to . . .

The article quoted John Withee:

> I've got a valuable gene bank here, the government tells me. The reason is simple—people won't correspond with the government. I get 20 letters a day from people who write and tell me about their latest leg fracture and then send me a packet of the family's heirloom beans.

Gardeners were willing to send seeds to other gardeners. The government seed lab was not set up to participate on that very human scale. In 1984, a duplicate of John's bean collection was sent to the National Seed Storage Lab in Colorado, giving the government a seed resource that in all likelihood it could never have collected itself.

An elderly woman once sent SSE some tomato seeds, saved for years from some that her grandmother had given her. She'd simply squirted the seeds, pulp, and juice onto a piece of newspaper. After the seeds had dried and pasted themselves to the paper, she folded it into a neat little square and sent it along. For her own garden, she picked the seed off the paper each spring to start her seedlings. What would the

The counter piled high with seeds in our living room office

government facility in Fort Collins have done had it received that tidy newspaper packet? The staff at the National Seed Storage Lab often forwarded correspondence and small samples of seeds from back yard gardeners to SSE; they seemed pleased to work with a grass-roots organization.

Meanwhile, Kent and I kept waiting for a slow moment to get caught up, but that moment never arrived. We could catch up on correspondence, but then the *Seed Savers Yearbook* would be published late. We needed another day in the week. Failing that, we needed to either cut back on our efforts for SSE or quit our day jobs, except for parenting.

Even though expanding Seed Savers was not about the money, there had to be enough money to pay for an expansion. SSE's revenues had exceeded expenses by no more than $3,000 over the previous three years—not even close to what was needed to grow, let alone sustain such growth.

Kent and I had managed to find jobs in the area to support our family and buy building materials for the house. We had minimal health insurance coverage—a policy with a large deductible but premiums of less than $100 a month. We paid as we could for the children's vaccinations and checkups.

Kent had worked at several jobs over the last few years—the night

Two-year-old
Tracy helping out
at Kent's desk

shift at a battery plant in Trenton, Missouri; the printing plant in Lamoni; the Missouri Department of Transportation. I had a part-time
job driving a small school bus to ferry children who lived on the gravel
roads near our house to the big bus on Route P. I was also a home
health aide, caring for elderly people.

We knew we could not continue to raise our family, handle our
jobs, finish our house, work our homestead, and develop SSE all at
the same time. Giving up parenting was not an option, and we had to
finish our house and cut wood before winter. Still, quitting our jobs
was quite a gamble.

Where was our business plan? Why didn't somebody stop us? Actually, our parents did try to give us valid reasons to keep our salaries.
But they had already failed to talk us out of homesteading in Missouri, so they gave up rather easily this time around. As the worrier in
the family—another trait inherited from my mother—I made a deal.
I insisted that there needed to be at least one year's financial cushion,
so we wouldn't starve. When we had that, I would be ready to make
the leap of faith.

Kent and I could not envision our life without Seed Savers. If we did not try to give 100 percent, we would never know what SSE could have been. The exchange had already encouraged gardeners all over the country and given them a forum to share their stories and their heirloom seeds. About 600 members had already offered about 3,000 heirloom or unusual vegetable varieties to more than 9,000 interested gardeners. We felt SSE had a tremendous responsibility— to the genetic diversity that was being lost in our food crops, to the future of the seeds, and to the histories of so many who had grown them.

SSE's compilation of seed was a living treasure. Unlike family jewels or furniture that only needed periodic cleaning, seeds had to be grown. Gardeners had entrusted Seed Savers Exchange with their families' heirlooms. To be a true steward of this resource, SSE had to ensure that this legacy lived beyond Kent and me. One legal entity in the United States capable of living beyond its founders is a nonprofit organization.

SSE had been incorporated for some time as a not-for-profit corporation in Missouri; in 1980, we applied for federal tax-exempt status. On March 19, 1981, Seed Savers Exchange Inc. was granted federal tax-exempt status under section 501(c) (3) of the Internal Revenue Code. Our grass-roots organization was now a legitimate tax-exempt corporation. Our board consisted of Kent, myself, and a friend who shared our vision, Gary Nabhan. Now we could accept grants and donations.

In December 1980, while the application was still pending, Kent applied for a grant for SSE from the Soil and Health Society in Emmaus, Pennsylvania, founded by J. I. Rodale and a forerunner of the Rodale Institute, known for its research into organic and sustainable farming practices. The application presented SSE's goals, which were simple and which still guide the organization today.

This was not a hobby for Kent and me anymore; it had become

our life's work. The grant would give Seed Savers Exchange the chance it needed to become self-supporting. We heard afterward that the late Robert Rodale, J. I. Rodale's son, wrote "5,000" in the margin of the proposal, and we got a check in the mail. In April, Kent quit his job.

We felt that if we could compile and publish a garden seed inventory, it would generate enough revenue to make SSE self-supporting. We had no business plan, just a worthy goal. Now we could really start to dream.

The Big Exposure

In 1981, Seed Savers Exchange had about sixty members and very little idea of what was happening in the broader world of seeds. We had always been focused on those who found us on their own. But one day Kent received a call from Mark Kane, a young writer for *Organic Gardening* magazine, which was published by Rodale.

I recently asked Mark how he discovered SSE. He said, "I had been receiving the mimeographed newsletters since early on and was fascinated with heirloom vegetables and seed-saving. I loved writing stories, useful stories, and had a gut instinct that there was something there. I pitched the idea to Lee Goldman, then the editor of *Organic Gardening*. He gave the go-ahead for a trip to northern Missouri and told me to take John Hammel, a photographer, with me."

Mark remembers calling us and said he could hear in Kent's voice how surprised and thrilled he was to know that SSE had caught the attention of someone beyond Missouri. "Please come," Kent said. He instructed Mark to fly to Kansas City and rent a car, apologized for not being able to put him up in our unfinished house, and said he would help find Mark a place to stay.

Recalling the trip, Mark laughed and said, "Hearing 'Kansas City' immediately had me fantasizing about barbecued ribs. I had always been a fan of Calvin Trillin, who was born and raised in Kansas City. Once, in a *Playboy* article, he branded Arthur Bryant's as the best restaurant in the world for barbecue. So after we arrived in KC, we rented a car without delay and headed to the legendary jazz quarter around 18th and Vine, a few blocks from Arthur Bryant's.

"We stepped into the restaurant, a dingy, narrow space filled with tables with cracked Formica tops and aluminum-tube chairs with ripped vinyl seats. A five-gallon jug of barbecue sauce was curing in the window, and looked like it had been there for a hundred years, or at least from when they opened in 1920. We stood in line at a Formica countertop, watched slow-cooking pork and ribs dripping juices into a pit below, placed our order, and pushed the cash payment through the half-moon opening in the plate glass.

"John suggested we order seven pounds of ribs. The ribs were weighed, wrapped in white wax-coated butcher paper, with a side of white bread, and we ate ribs all the way to Princeton."

Much as Calvin Trillin's *Playboy* article continues to draw attention to Arthur Bryant's, the *Organic Gardening* article led to publicity we still receive today. The magazine had a readership of 1.2 million in 1981, and Mark wrote a terrific story. Whether Mark and John came to Missouri for ribs or for Seed Savers Exchange, the result was the beginning of SSE's big exposure.

Getting Together

By 1981, Seed Savers Exchange was beginning to thrive. The volume of members, seeds offered, seeds sent to the exchange, and correspondence was increasing. So far our face-to-face contact with members had been limited to a few visitors who found us after taking the bus to

Bethany. Kent and I wanted to see members' faces and hear them tell stories in their own voices. We were curious about this special group of gardeners who were keeping heirloom seeds. What did they have in common? Why did they save seeds?

Our plan for a small, informal gathering gave rise to a little angst. I had three children to keep track of—the baby, Tracy, was a year old—in addition to organizing the weekend. What would I make for meals? Our gardens would have to be full of heirloom plants, weed-free and healthy. Our house wasn't finished. Would we run out of water?

When campout weekend arrived, June 13 and 14, 1981, twelve people had confirmed their attendance. We sent maps to everyone so they could find us and a proviso to bring tents, seeds, and children. (A map was a necessity in the days before GPS: Visitors drove on blacktop for nine miles and then took four different gravel roads to our house.) The inside of the house was pretty rough—plastic still covered the

Campout attendees meeting on the unfinished white oak deck at the Whealys' Missouri homestead

windows, so we couldn't open them. But the unfinished white oak deck on the east side of our house overlooked a meadow of wild daisies in bloom and miles of river bottom—a lovely place to gather. We focused our available construction time on the deck and pounded the last nail the morning of the first day of the first Campout Convention of the Seed Savers Exchange.

By late morning on June 13, Russell Crow, a bean collector from Illinois, had arrived. He was followed in swift succession by Faxon and Mary Stinnett of Oklahoma; Virgil

Mary Stinnett, Clarice Cooper, Hazel Johnson, Diane Ott Whealy, and Mary Razor working up a batch of peas for the campout dinner

and Hazel Johnson from Missouri; and then all at once: Auburn and Clarice Cooper from Kansas, Tom and Sue Knoche from Ohio, Dale Anderson and his nephew Rex from Indiana; and Al and Mary Razor from Iowa. We'd never seen so many cars in our driveway—and from so far afield.

We gathered together for a potluck lunch and didn't stop talking until it came time to say goodbye to our new friends at the end of the weekend. During one lull in activity, Mary Stinnett volunteered to help out with the pea picking for Saturday's supper. Bless her sweet heart! She organized the other women and soon we were podding, shelling, hulling—whatever you call it—a bumper crop of Lincoln peas at the peak of perfection. We had an appreciative audience that night.

Also for the evening meal on our new deck, we barbecued chicken on our green square Weber grill. After eating, we relaxed until the mosquitoes came out, then continued the conversations inside. Fax was a wonderful storyteller. The night was clear and the stars were brilliant, with no lights for miles to interfere. Frogs were croaking by our little pond behind the house and whippoorwills were so close we

The first campout,
June 1981

could hear them catch their breath between calls. Everyone pitched tents in the yard or stayed in their campers, except for Tom and Sue, who had a motel room at the Wagon Wheel in town. Aaron and Amy at first felt disappointed that there were no children to play with, but they got into the spirit when Kent pitched their pup tent in the yard so they, too, could camp out.

The next morning, over coffee and homemade cinnamon rolls, the best seed trading in the country took place. Clarice brought Grandpa Edmonson's cucumber seed. Mary Razor brought her grandmother's tansy. Dale brought his Grandmother Boyer's greens, a perennial dock-like plant. Fax had a collection of more than one hundred different tomato varieties. He also had pepper seeds and was especially proud of the hot yellow peppers called Yoyo. They had been given to him by a Native American woman, but he'd also heard they were called squash peppers in eastern Texas. Tom brought squash seed; Russ and Virgil talked beans.

After the *Organic Gardening* article came out, readers had started to send us letters with samples of their own beans, seeking identification. On Sunday morning of the campout we decided to put Russ's and Virgil's expertise to work, watching and listening as they went through the letters and offered their opinions on identification. We could not have hired live entertainment more enjoyable.

For Sunday dinner, I had assembled my reliable lasagna recipe with homemade tomato sauce ahead of time. There was salad of Grandpa Admire's lettuce and a cobbler with frozen wild black raspberries—blackcaps, we called them. Cooking, I guess, was in my DNA; maybe I inherited the "cooking for a threshing crew" gene from my mother. We had plenty of food, and we didn't run out of water.

Kent and I were pleased with our first effort to bring people together. Those who attended that year expressed surprise that such strong friendships could develop in just two days. Everyone had a hard time saying goodbye, and some tears were shed. "I have never met anyone in my life that I could talk to about my collection of seed," Tom Knoche said. "I always gardened with my granny and we saved seeds. No one else ever would have understood or shared my excitement. Not too many folks are interested anymore."

About a week later, Kent and I received an encouraging letter from Dale Anderson. Dale was excited and energized by the weekend—and deeply appreciative of our hospitality. He thought there was nothing we Whealys couldn't do with the Exchange. Reading his kind words reinforced our feeling that the path we were on was leading to nothing but good, and nothing would stop us now.

Customized hubcap wheel cover for the 1983 campout

The Campouts Catch On

The second SSE campout convention was held on June 12 and 13, 1982. By then our house had windows and we had a fourth child, Carrie,

born February 28. It was Year Six of our homesteading, and I was starting to measure time in unusual increments. Our family was looking forward to seeing our seed-saving friends from the previous year.

Fax and Mary Stinnett brought small gifts, read books to the girls, and stocked candy in their camper for any little visitors. Mary once gave me a green Frankoma pottery trivet that I still treasure. Dale Anderson and the Stinnetts became our children's honorary grandparents.

With a baby and three older children, my time was definitely split in many ways that year. Sue Knoche, who raised six children of her own, offered to help with the girls and I gladly accepted.

Faxon Stinnett
reading to Tracy

At that campout and future ones, Sue made certain that Amy, Tracy, and Carrie had whatever they needed—baths, snacks, and plenty of attention. My adult daughters still have tender memories of her. Tracy says, "Sue had a Southern accent that was soothing and she made us feel important. I just loved her!"

Seedy characters
inside

Carl Barnes
discussing corn
varieties while
Mark Fox, sitting
at the picnic table,
studies a particular
sample of corn seed

For the second campout, I'd decided to enlist the help of Beth
Wileman, who'd owned a restaurant in town and recently retired.
Not only was the food excellent, but she and her husband delivered
all the meals. (My friend Ronna in Princeton still sees Beth at church
each Sunday, and asked her if she remembered that campout. Beth replied, "Oh yes, that was fun, but I had a terrible time with the custard
filling in that special layer cake they ordered.")

We had thirty-five seed savers at our second campout, so attendance had tripled. It was still a very informal affair with no set schedule or roster of speakers. Carl Barnes and his wife, Karen, came from
Oklahoma with a display of Native American corns the likes of which
none of us had ever seen. He was inundated with "oohs" and "ahs" and
questions but took it all in stride. And Russ Crow brought an artful
display of beans that was much appreciated by all, especially by heirloom bean lover Mark Fox and his wife, Beth, and their children, Ian
and Carrie.

The Klines' teepee set up in the middle of the circle drive

The Klines from Minnesota drove up with sixteen-foot poles and a roll of canvas strapped to the top of their car. They set up a glorious teepee in the middle of our circle drive; inside was a very irritable Siamese cat, which made the teepee a double curiosity for the kids. But everyone was warned not to enter.

On June 11 and 12, 1983, we held our third annual gathering with fifty seed savers in attendance from far and wide. We had now formed a close-knit community of friends who felt like family.

The house was certainly not big enough to host that many seed savers. Our cistern held only five hundred gallons of water and everyone used our bathroom. I woke up Sunday morning to the constant running of the water pump, the unmistakable signal of an empty cistern. We had to make an emergency call to Eddie Sims, the water hauler, to bring a tank. Carl Barnes passed the hat for the $30 load.

But Kent and I were energized by this evidence of interest in seed-saving, and were more determined than ever to follow our instincts. So far we'd created four children and started an organization that had preserved 3,500 seeds in the central collection (2,000 beans, 500 peppers, 200 squashes, 140 corns, 100 muskmelons, 100 potatoes, 100 peas, and sundry others). We never doubted—or cared—that our life was growing out of control.

Moon and Stars Watermelon

Kent and I had been together for seven years before we thought about having a television set in our home. We were living in Great-Aunt Hazel's house outside Princeton, and building our own house, and there was always something to work on or something to read. But we thought Aaron and Amy would appreciate some interaction with the outside world, even if it was just Bert and Ernie on *Sesame Street*. So we used our tax refund to purchase a nineteen-inch color portable Zenith.

With no antenna, we quickly discovered we could get reception from only KTVO in Kirksville, a locally owned station with a limited budget. The kids watched *Sesame Street*; we watched agricultural news, local programming, and the *PTL Club*.

In the spring of 1981 we got a call from Ron Heller, who hosted the agriculture news segment on KTVO. He wanted an interview about SSE. We agreed, of course, and Ron and his crew came to the house. Kent and Ron sat in oak chairs in front of our granite fireplace, and for about ten minutes Kent explained what we were doing. Tracy and Amy were sitting on the marble hearth, happily playing with a small bucket of dried beans. Just as the camera crew panned in to get a shot of the girls, Tracy dumped the whole pail of beans over Amy's head. Cut!

Near the end of the interview, Ron asked whether there were any seeds SSE members had been unable to locate. Kent told him about Moon and Stars watermelon, a particularly striking species. Both the oval melon and its foliage are deep green, covered with bright yellow blotches of various sizes—the stars and moons. The seed had been offered during the 1930s by Henry Fields in Shenandoah, Iowa, and the

Kent with Moon and Stars watermelon at Van Dorens' farm

Robinson Seed Company in Waterloo, Nebraska, he told Ron, and added that we hoped the seed hadn't been lost.

After the show aired, SSE received a dozen or so letters and phone calls from area residents who either had older seed or were looking for some family favorite they used to grow and had somehow lost. One special letter was from Merle Van Doren, who lived about a hundred miles southeast of Princeton. "My dad always grew Moon and Stars in Tennessee and I have grown the melon on my farm near Macon for as long as I can remember," Merle wrote. "The melon is like the Black Diamond but more disease-resistant. The fruit usually matures in about 90 days. I will save some seed for you."

That fall, *Mother Earth News* sent two staff members, Jeanne Malmgren and Larry Hollar (who later became president of Hollar Seeds), to our house to talk to Kent for a regular feature they called a "Plowboy Interview." They took advantage of the opportunity to accompany the Whealy family to Merle Van Doren's farm. The melon patch was behind the Van Dorens' farmhouse, and a mound of about ten melons had been placed on the lawn in front of the garden. The bright yellow moons and stars glowed against the grass, with a background of yellow marigolds and a few red velvet cockscomb peeking out for contrast. I don't think any designer could have staged a more beautiful shot. Merle declined to be photographed, but Jeanne took a photo of Kent looking very pleased.

The afternoon ended around the Van Dorens' kitchen table with a modest lunch of fresh tomatoes and open-faced pimento loaf sandwiches—and of course slices of Moon and Stars watermelon. Then Kent and I loaded the car with as many watermelons as we could cram in, and drove back to our homestead feeling as if we had found a pot of gold. The Whealy family enjoyed a lot of watermelon that fall, under the policy that you could eat all you wanted, but you had to keep the seeds.

"I'm sure some folk would give a pretty penny to get their hands on this melon seed," Merle had said, but when Kent told him he was just going to give it away to as many people as he could, Merle grinned. They both knew that the seed had financial value but agreed that the best arrangement was to freely distribute it to as many gardeners as possible.

The Exchange sent samples to more than one hundred members. In the second edition of the *Garden Seed Inventory*, printed in 1988, a few commercial sources were already offering Moon and Stars and, by 2004, when the sixth edition came out, there were more than four dozen commercial sources for Moon and Stars and its variants. Today, heirloom seed catalogs offer many different strains of Moon and Stars watermelon, including Long Milky Way, but our family favorite will always be the one from the Van Dorens' farm.

The Wanigan Associates

In the 1960s, while Kent and I were still exploring, John Withee was collecting seeds for our future. John had founded a nonprofit organization called the Wanigan Associates, devoted to the preservation of heirloom bean varieties. *Wanigan* is the Abnaki Indian word for "kitchens mounted on rafts," which would ply the rivers of Maine

during the spring lumber drives. Huge quantities of beans were cooked in these floating kitchens and served to Maine woodsmen.

After corresponding with John, we finally met him at the Seed Banks Serving People Workshop, in Tucson, Arizona, in October 1981. The workshop brought together people interested in preserving plant diversity and genetic conservation. The enthusiasm we encountered there sustained Kent and me and reinforced SSE's mission to save seeds.

"In Massachusetts, when I got a piece of land big enough to have a fire in the back yard," John told the workshop, "I decided to revive my family's tradition of cooking beans in the ground. When I was a youngster, it was my job on Fridays to clean out the hole, start the fire, and get the rocks hot. Then my mother would have the pot of beans ready and we'd drop them into the ground on Friday night and the whole family would eat them on Saturday.

"I went to the local stores in Massachusetts for my supply of beans and didn't find certain ones I remembered, like Jacob's Cattle bean. So I went back home to Maine and began my hobby, this 'collecting.' The first thing I knew I had as many as 50 varieties, which was unheard of. It kept going like that until the number was getting up pretty large [about 1,200 varieties] and I had to worry about how I was going to keep them alive.

"Then I dreamed up this retirement scheme," he told us. He pro-

duced a small seed catalog that he then sent to a mailing list consisting
of people who had replied to his notices in free publications. Kent and
I looked at each other and thought: This is really sounding familiar.

Help! My House Is Full of Beans

Not many folks ventured down the dirt roads in northern Mercer
County, Missouri. The peacefulness surrounding our house might
sound idyllic, but sometimes I felt lonely. Today I'd call that a sign of
homesteader fatigue. At the first sound of gravel grinding under a car's
wheels, we got excited.

One day, a UPS truck stopped on the circle drive in front of our
house, and the driver shouted from his window, "You guys sure do live
out in the country. I'm glad I found you way back here." He unloaded
three large boxes and Kent signed his log. And then the truck left in
a cloud of dust.

Amy was excited. "What did he bring us?" she asked. Kent answered, "Lots of beans!" I sensed her disappointment, but she was
still curious: "Who sent them to us?" The beans had come from John
Withee, who'd asked Seed Savers Exchange to take over the Wanigan collection. Kent and I were pleased that John had trusted SSE
with his collection. We understood how difficult it was for him to let
go, and we also understood how difficult it had been to get the seeds
ready for the trip to Missouri.

SSE had formed a relationship with Rodale Research Center
(originally founded in 1949 as the Soil and Health Society) because
of a shared interest in sustainable crops. In the summer of 1981, Peggy
Haas and four young women from the research center went to John's
house in Maine, threshed beans, answered correspondence, and got
the Wanigan beans organized. They split the collection into three

Sorted beans
in labeled jars

duplicate sets: one stayed with John, one went to the Rodale Research Center, and one went to SSE. This first delivery of boxes contained 1,185 samples of beans and accession records for each variety. John always stressed the importance of good record-keeping.

The evening of the big bean delivery, after the children were in bed, Kent and I sat in the living room with the boxes. John's lifelong love and collection were spending the night on the living room floor. I had a sobering but wonderful thought and said, "The Wanigan beans are now part of the SSE family." John had given us a tremendous gift, and a tremendous responsibility.

Three large boxes of beans were manageable, but the bean situation got worse—or better, depending on how you view it. In the spring of 1983, John decided to give SSE the rest of his beans. The Rodale crew packed all of them—shelled beans, unshelled beans, beans in packages, beans in letters, beans in jars—into thirty-three sturdy cartons and shipped them to SSE. After seeing how much was delivered, Kent thought it could be the contents of all John's seed sheds. And earlier that week we'd already received about 300 smaller boxes of beans from the SSE Growers' Network.

Our road had become quite familiar to the UPS driver. And the Whealy house was filling up with beans.

John had never wanted to store his beans in opaque plastic containers, and we were of the same opinion, especially after we saw the beauty of these bean seeds. If it wasn't illegal to hide those wondrous colors, it certainly was immoral. Luckily for us, a Seed Savers member from Florida named James Eagle worked in a hospital and had access to empty half-pint infant formula bottles with airtight lids. He offered to ship them. Soon 3,000 bottles arrived at the door, and the project continued to escalate.

We definitely needed more space. The previous spring, I'd had a garage sale in the Princeton Community Center, and thought perhaps we could rent that space for Operation Bean Rescue. The large basement was available and we hauled all the beans to town in a farm truck the same day that a tractor-trailer truck delivered 140 cases of bottles from Florida.

We found some volunteer help in the person of Russ Crow of Woodstock, Illinois. A bean collector and one of SSE's first members, Russ worked the night shift at a Chrysler plant, but had recently been in an auto accident. A week or so before the beans arrived, Kent talked to Russ, who reported that he had broken a few ribs and would be off work for a month to recover. "He said he was just sitting around the house bored," Kent said.

I had a sudden thought: "Do you think he would come to Missouri to help out?" Kent pondered that. "We could always ask. Maybe if we offered to buy his bus ticket and gave him free room and board he might." Russ agreed to help with the rescue and stayed with us for two weeks.

Custom-made
wooden bean cases

Slowly, "lots of beans" were transformed into a useable collection.
Kent and Russ started shelling, cleaning, sorting, and labeling. They
filled 2,200 jars and 2,500 packets of bean seeds. The Wanigan bean
collection was under control and ready to return to our house.

We knew we had more than 1,200 different beans, but it was just
a number. The colors in those beans—bronze, gold, brown, burgundy,
red, yellow—and their speckled markings are impossible to describe.
The beans were to be housed in our basement, in five handsome
wooden seed cases made by Jim Schooler, a woodworker who was
a friend from Princeton. The cases were ten drawers high and each
drawer held eighty bottles of beans.

(Those cases are still with SSE. They moved with us later to Decorah, Iowa, then were stored in various basements and garages, before taking up residence in a small gift shop in the barn at Heritage

Farm. Visitors still remember opening those drawers of beans. Today we use the empty drawers for drying seed. After our tomatoes are squeezed and processed, we place the seeds on coffee filters in deli tubs, and put them in the drawers to finish drying.)

Jim also made two traveling displays that resembled large wooden suitcases; each opened like a book, displaying two large pages of beans. The cases held 800 different varieties from the Wanigan collection, side by side in square-inch boxes covered with clear glass. They reminded me of my Grandma Einck's postage-stamp quilt, but instead of cloth blocks there were squares of calico-colored beans. It was the most diverse patchwork quilt imaginable. Jim made one for John and one for SSE. John's case and its contents are now in the Peabody Museum in Salem, Massachusetts.

Today, Seed Savers has more than 5,000 different bean varieties; the heart of this collection came from John Withee, who died in 1993, and the Wanigan Associates.

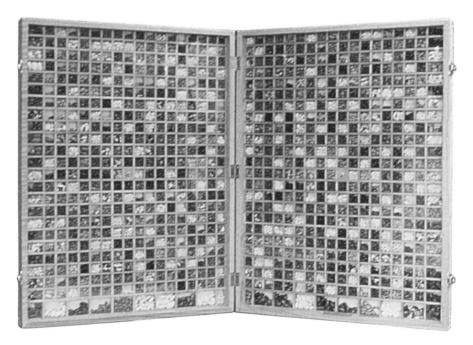

Traveling bean display holding 800 different varieties from the Wanigan collection

The Garden Seed Inventory

The seeds that first inspired SSE were family heirlooms. But many nonhybrid vegetable varieties offered by mail-order commercial seed companies were also being lost. (Both family heirlooms and commercial nonhybrid seeds are rich in genetic diversity and often irreplaceable.)

Many gardeners thought that hybrid seeds were new and improved, and who wouldn't want that? But as customers flocked to the hybrid varieties, seed companies found older standard varieties less desirable. In the seed business, as in most business ventures, it doesn't make sense to maintain inventory that's not selling. Besides, from the seed sellers' standpoint, there was an advantage to hybrids: gardeners could not keep the seeds from year to year, because the seed of hybrids are unreliable, or revert back to one of the plant parents. As a result, customers had to reorder seed every year.

At the same time, many small family-owned seed companies with a regional focus were being bought out by larger corporate owners. The corporations had little interest in low-profit, regionally adapted varieties that sold modestly; for the most part, the corporations replaced these cultivars with all-purpose hybrid vegetables or new patented varieties. It was believed that these varieties would sell to a wider audience because they adapted to different growing conditions.

SSE could monitor the situation by compiling an inventory of nonhybrid seed still offered by the U.S. and Canadian garden-seed industry. Then gardeners could easily identify endangered varieties, order them, and maintain them. But the thought of beginning another major project, while trying to keep up with the usual SSE demands, was daunting. Were we overextending ourselves?

Many scientists whom we respected encouraged us to compile such an inventory. For more than a decade, these scientists had been warning about the dangerous consequences of losing genetic diversity. We decided to proceed.

Kent wrote an SSE grant application to the Jessie Smith Noyes Foundation for $8,000, and part of the grant was used to purchase a computer system. We set it up in Aaron's bedroom, and that's where Kent spent most of the next three years. It seemed as if he came out of the room only to eat or sleep. He wrote later: "Diane would stick her head in the door of the room where I was working on the inventory and say, 'You know, the baby is almost three.'"

On the day that baby was born, I went to Kent's makeshift office and said, "I think it's time to get to the hospital." He continued to type. Then he looked up and saw me clenching the doorframe. "Let's go!" he said.

Our life was like homesteading. We thought the inventory would be completed within a year and list 120 seed catalogs offering 3,000 nonhybrid varieties. The *Garden Seed Inventory* took three times that long to finish. It listed 239 companies and nearly 6,000 nonhybrid varieties.

The book came out to enthusiastic reviews. The cover carried a blurb from the late Robert Rodale, then editor of *Organic Gardening*, who called the inventory "a sharp tool for the actions that many people need to take to preserve the base of genetic diversity on which our food system rests." There were kudos from Wendell Berry, Carolyn Jabs, Roger B. Swain, Garrison Wilkes, and Nancy Bubel.

Starting in 1984, when the inventory was partly completed, Seed Savers Exchange began purchasing endangered varieties from commercial catalogs and then maintaining them for the central collection. Eventually, using profits from the sale of the book, SSE made it a practice to order seed of every variety offered by only one company, on the grounds that if the variety were dropped the next year, it would be too late to get it into our collection.

We didn't have to go far to see the value of an inventory illustrated. My mother had long ordered and planted Empress, a snap bean, from Gurney's. In the late 1980s, she placed her seed order as usual, but when she received her package, Empress was stamped "no longer available" on the packing slip. She telephoned Gurney's (a big deal at the time, because long-distance calls were costly) to see if by chance they still had some seed on hand. A helpful customer service employee explained that the bean, first named Experimental Bean 121, was renamed Empress when it became popular in 1979. But demand for the seed had decreased, and when all the seed was sold out, sometimes even the stock seed, the bean was dropped from the catalog.

Kent and I checked the SSE collection and found Empress bean, snap bush bean, source Gurney's. I don't think we could have given my mom a better gift for Mother's Day than Empress bean seed. We hoped our success story was duplicated many times.

Well Rooted, a Dream Grows

Kent and I never stopped dreaming or talking about SSE. All of the Whealys literally lived in the middle of our work. In addition to the computer in Aaron's bedroom, Kent's desk in the living room always overflowed with piles of mail and boxes of seed. We started each day with seed-saving conversations over coffee and ended each day discussing a letter or our garden, or scheming about how we could make all this work. The kids, who were forced to hear about seed-saving day and night, were unbelievably patient.

When we visited Kent's family in Wellington, we stayed on I-35 most of the way, but sometimes drove around Kansas City or took back roads. One spring, Aaron and Amy told us we could not talk about work on the entire trip. Kent and I promised no seed-savers talk and innocently admired the hillsides. At that time of year, most trees were still winter gray. But the delicate twigs from the redbud trees were like fireworks, lighting up hillsides with scarlet starbursts.

The southwest route around Kansas City was hilly, and renowned for its well-groomed horse ranches. Up and down, mile after mile, we drove by horse farms, their stables used for boarding, training, and breeding. Ponds with grass-covered dams riffled white in the spring gusts. White board fences surrounded pastures and lined driveways leading to magnificent barns and houses surrounded by beds of daffodils or hyacinths. Behind the fences, horses of chestnut, sorrel, black, palomino, white, gray, and dun reminded us of calico beans sprinkled on a green blanket.

We had kept our pledge to the kids until that point, but when Kent and I realized that we felt the same energy and shared the same thought, we started dreaming out loud. What if Seed Savers Exchange owned a farm nestled into rolling hills, with white board fences lining the drive toward beautiful gardens planted with diverse crops of vegetables? It could have a modest farmhouse, a barn to house rare breeds, perhaps a pond . . .

We had already recognized the need to have a place to grow the seed collection and keep the seeds viable. But that day we envisioned a showplace—a farm where SSE members could visit, walk through gardens, see and taste the genetic diversity we continuously talked about, and feel the same sense of awe. Despite our best efforts for the sake of the children, we spilled over with ideas and possibilities for most of the trip to Wellington. I understood that this beautiful dream might be an impossible one, but it was too late to stop thinking about it. The dream had been planted.

Moving to Iowa

After our trip to Kansas, we returned to Missouri energized by our vision of a display farm. We knew if SSE was to become a destination, we had to relocate to a more populated area. Seed Savers—and the Whealys—would have to move.

Other factors made Missouri less appealing. The growing conditions were not suitable for large gardening; our ridge had poor soil and not enough groundwater to support an irrigation system. Our home had to serve as office, seed warehouse, and gathering spot for events.

About three dozen people attended the third campout in 1983, and our home was no longer large enough. It was a twenty-two-mile round trip on bad roads to town. And the whole family, on various levels, was feeling the need to get away from constant seclusion. (Charlie and Val had already succumbed and moved back west in 1979.) Better to move soon, we reasoned, than wait for the organization to grow even bigger—which would further complicate the move.

Our list of criteria for the new home was quite different from our homesteading requirements. The farm needed to be conveniently located, with good growing conditions, schools, roads, drinking water, medical facilities, stores for goods and groceries, including a food co-op. Preferably there would be a small liberal arts college, restaurants, and a movie theater, and the town would be concerned with historical preservation. And yes, a river should run through it.

The town we were considering was Decorah, Iowa, population 8,000, located in the very northeast corner of the state. I had grown up about twenty miles south of Decorah, and we never watered our crops. My parents grew a large family garden and productive fields of corn, oats, and alfalfa. Kent, too, was impressed by the fertility of the land.

When we went to visit my parents, Decorah was our favorite place to explore. We admired the idyllic dairy farms in the area, the vibrant downtown, the Oneota Food Co-op, the historic district, Luther College, and, as a cultural bonus, Vesterheim, the most comprehensive Norwegian museum in the country. The Upper Iowa River (great for canoeing and tubing) flowed swiftly through the parks and down through the middle of town.

While much of Iowa is flat and planted with corn and soybeans, Decorah is surrounded by dramatic limestone bluffs, caves, and swift cold streams that flow both above ground and below. The town has thirteen city parks and twenty-five miles of trout streams and hiking trails. On one of those trails, on our way to see Malanaphy Springs tumbling off a rock ledge into the river, we were overwhelmed by hillsides covered with bluebells. One Memorial Day we found plump morel mushrooms growing in a tiny crack of soil between limestone steps leading into Ice Cave. The children were most enthusiastic about living close to their grandparents' farm, Mabe's Pizza, and a soft-serve ice cream stand called the Whippy Dip.

I know you may be thinking we were lured to Decorah by morels, lefsa, and lutefisk, but actually it was the Schultz Kiln. In 1983, during a Thanksgiving visit, we drove through the historic district up to Phelps Park. The park is fifty-six acres with fountains, rock walls, paths, and gazebos all overlooking the river, the valley, and town. In the park was a fallen-down kiln built in 1870 and used to fire the brick

Thousands of letters from all over the world were delivered to R.R. 2, Princeton, Missouri

for most of Decorah's original buildings. After the last bricks were fired in the 1920s, the city took over the kiln for tool storage, but its dome of bricks eventually fell into disrepair. Faced with the choice of tearing it down or restoring it, Decorah chose preservation. Kent and I both related to the idea of preserving history.

Back in Missouri, our family debated the decision all summer. One hot afternoon, we decided to go on a picnic at Nine Eagles State Park. The park had a lake with a sand beach leading to a shallow swimming area. When we were done with our picnic, the conversation, as usual, turned to whether or not we should move to Decorah. Kent took a penny from his pocket and said, "I'm tired of this. Heads we move to Decorah; tails we don't."

He flipped the coin into the air, but missed the catch, and the penny rolled out of sight down the bank toward the lake. We could see the copper one-cent piece down below us, stuck in the mud exactly on edge. We all groaned. But then when Kent asked what everyone wanted it to be, we all said, "Heads!" Aaron added, "I want to go to the movies." So the decision was made—we would move to Decorah.

Leaving Our Homestead

I know that Rome wasn't built in a day and that the great cathedrals of Europe took centuries to complete, but I never would have thought that building a simple family house could take eight years.

Still, we had a sturdy, unique house that used mostly native wood, including walnut, maple, sycamore, and oak, the bulk of it cut from our property. Tender, loving care had gone into building the granite fireplace and other fine features. The house was gorgeous and we were proud of what we'd accomplished.

But we hired Jim Schooler, our woodworker friend, to build the

The finished Whealy homestead house, 1984

front porch and add the finishing touches. We had to finish the house so we could sell it. My heart would not have been broken if we'd left an unfinished house, but to leave our finished house was hard. We did get to enjoy it for a few months, in a bittersweet way.

The rewards of the time we spent as a family in Missouri were immeasurable. Kent, Aaron, and Amy took satisfaction in writing their names in the fresh mortar beside the date, 1979, when the last granite stone for the fireplace was laid. Our family grew closer in the isolation of northern Missouri, and the solitude also gave SSE a chance to be nurtured. We moved on with a sense of accomplishment and a renewed spirit of adventure.

We needed to find a buyer who would appreciate the unusual details of our handmade house and overlook the lack of roads and reliably safe drinking water. Well water was not an option where we lived, for irrigation or for household use. The groundwater was deep and wells were expensive. And if you were lucky enough to hit water, it had so much iron that it was orange—not appetizing to drink, useless for laundry, and corrosive on pipes.

We set a selling price that covered the cost of the land and the materials used in the house, but none of our labor. And we quickly learned that finding a buyer even at that price was next to impossible. We ended up renting the house for two years before we could sell it.

Eight years earlier, we'd moved to Missouri in a short-bed pickup truck. But now we had all the homesteading gear we moved then, four children, 4,000 varieties of seed from SSE's collection, four 6-foot-tall solid-oak bean cases and more than 2,000 bottles of beans SSE got from John Withee, file cabinets full of correspondence, boxes of seed catalogs, a computer, and a cute Beagle puppy. This time, we needed a large U-Haul truck.

The stove and refrigerator were loaded into the front of the U-Haul a few days before we left. I was trying not to accumulate perishables. The last day we survived on canned peaches, Girl Scout cookies, coffee, and milk. Even today I'm reminded of our move whenever I taste a Girl Scout Thin Mint.

On February 28, 1984, our daughter Carrie's second birthday, we finished loading the truck, save for a couple of mattresses that we could load in the morning. I didn't sleep well that night, not because we were on the floor, but because I knew it was the last time our family would be under that roof. But the next morning the sun was shining brightly on a thin layer of frost that coated the trees and hillsides. Pokey the puppy jumped into the front seat of the truck alongside Amy and Carrie. Aaron and Tracy would start the trip with me, in the car.

As we drove around the circle drive and headed down the road, I unexpectedly got teary. "Mom, are you going to cry all the way to Iowa?" Aaron asked. I replied, "I really don't know."

Twenty-five years later, on a recent trip back to Princeton, I arranged to meet with the current owners of our house, Melvin and Sue Stotts, who bought it from the people we sold it to. Area residents, Melvin told me, still say the house was "done different." He added, "I have never seen a house built so strong. You must have thought when a tornado hit you wanted the whole house to go together." I had to laugh when his stepson, Ray Lewis, recalled repair projects: "Nothing in that house is normal!"

Sue said she was ecstatic to have found the house. "I was working on the pre-Census in 1989 and drove way back here. I could not believe my eyes, this house was everything I ever dreamt about. As luck would have it, the house became available for sale shortly after that time. I felt like my prayers had been answered." She said that she'd often told others: "God has sent these people here to build this perfect place for me."

That seemed a bit unrealistic. But knowing that our home was loved and that all its little details were appreciated made me happy. Melvin was also a collector of fossils and most proud of his Hopewell artifacts, which were all found in the dried Weldon River bottom on the property. He displayed his collection in a glass case in the living room, where we once showcased SSE's colorful seed collection.

First Iowa Campouts

In the spring of 1984, we needed to find a place near Decorah to hold the fourth annual Seed Savers Exchange campout. As a girl I'd belonged to the Festina Starlets 4-H club (the boys were the Festina Stars). Every summer we'd attended Pine Bluff 4-H camp, on the river road about eight miles northeast of Decorah. The camp is located on 115 acres of pine-covered bluffs, with a narrow suspension bridge leading over the Upper Iowa River to trails. There were four cabins lined with bunk beds, restrooms, showers, a big kitchen with plenty of water, and a large shelter house that covered picnic tables used for meetings and meals.

My mother's sister, Lorraine Schrandt, and her friend Phyllis Jackson, who had cooked for weddings and church events, agreed to prepare the meals for $6 an hour. They were the best. Aunt Lorraine and Phyllis could put together any traditional Iowa dish in large quantities. We decided to barbecue about thirty chickens for Saturday evening. I was to make two gallons of my catsup-based barbecue sauce, a recipe that I picked up from a friend when we lived in Kansas. We would serve the usual side dishes: homemade potato salad, fresh coleslaw, and home-baked bread.

My mother could easily have cooked for the whole event, but her health wasn't good enough. She lent a hand peeling and thinly slicing potatoes for the salad and cabbage for the slaw—cabbage and potatoes provided by my parents. On the picnic tables, she placed bowls of her canned pickled beets and fruit jars with spikes of tall red, white, and coral gladiolas cut from her flower bed. Dad picked up fresh eggs for the potato salad for 35 cents a dozen and bought several pounds of butter from the Festina Creamery.

Phyllis made her specialty, raisin bread pudding with hard sauce, which called for "whiskey to taste." When I asked her for the recipe, she grabbed a pencil and wrote on a piece of yellow lined paper. I have carried her instructions with me for nearly thirty years in a red tin box that also holds recipes cut from newspapers and magazines, sent to me in letters, or written on 3 × 5 index cards, envelopes, napkins, or bank deposit slips.

My daughters ask me why I don't organize the recipes into categories, or make them into computer files so I don't have to look through the whole box each time. But that tin is a scrapbook of food memories. As I leaf through the box looking for the bread pudding recipe, I remember Kent's grandmother when I find the recipe for Nana's farm pickles. When I read Mom's recipe for butterscotch pie, I'm back in her kitchen smelling burnt sugar. And I chuckle at Grandma Einck's handwritten annotation on her oyster stew recipe—"good if you like it"—and her spelling of "cocoanut."

I eventually do come across the paper with Phyllis's handwriting, creased from folding and refolding. I've read it many times over the years, always with the same thought: "Oh, that was so good. I'll make it soon." But I never have.

I also have Aunt Lorraine's recipe for potato salad. The first ingredient is 10 pounds of potatoes.

Steve Neal and Tom Knoche swapping seeds

We didn't set out to eat locally and organically. It was just the way this small community cooperated. There was pride in growing fresh vegetables and preparing a wonderful meal with simple ingredients. But the weekend of that first Iowa campout, something new was added: these women were noticed and appreciated by people outside the community. In the Festina vicinity, these ordinary meals have always been respected but taken for granted. The surprise on the cooks' faces when they were complimented was a sweet testament to their humility.

The large limestone fireplace in the shelter house was the meeting spot for our Saturday night brainstorming sessions. Seed savers gathered at the picnic tables for conversations about their successes and failures in the garden and about improving their growing records, description lists, seed purity, and storage.

Tom Knoche, who had attended the first campout in Missouri, was hoping to unravel a mystery in his garden: Which of the eight different roasting squashes he grew was the true old Cherokee squash

Carl Barnes,
John Hartman, and
Virgil Johnson at the
4-H camp, Decorah

called Candy Roaster? The topic changed to beans, and Tom said:
"My granny said all her life that no bean was worth eating unless you
had to string it first." And there were discussions about the relative age
of varieties—Lazy Housewife bean was old, it was agreed, but Scotia
Cornfield and the Cutshorts were much older.

After dark, Mark Widrlechner, a horticulturist at the USDA's
Plant Introduction Station at Iowa State University, and his wife,
Sherry Dragula, showed slides of their work with ornamental corns.
People began giving short speeches about their personal preservation
projects. Discussions continued late into the night on how to help
small seed companies, the Growers' Network, and SSE keep up with
its recent growth. And, as usual, collectors brought their seeds for
trading. Chickens were barbecued; guitars and harmonicas played in
the background, and Mark Fox photographed it all.

Every one of the original campers from Missouri came to the first
Iowa campout, and there were sixty new campers. Before the weekend
was over, we "founding campers" realized how much we missed seeing
each other and catching up. It was decided that in 1985, those who had
attended the first two campouts in Missouri would meet in the back
room of the Café Deluxe, a Decorah restaurant, at 1 o'clock on Friday,

before the rest of the weekend started. We called it the Old Timers' Lunch. That tradition continued for many years, until sadly we lost many of the original campers. We cherish their spirit, enthusiasm, and expertise. And each year we're joined by a whole new cast of seed fanatics and collectors.

We had already made a connection with Glenn Drowns, and more people with special interests and skills found SSE as well. Ted Gibbs with his okra collection; Gary Nabhan with Native American crops, squash, and melons; our dear friend Thane Earle with tomatoes; John Swenson, who was recently named an honorary SSE board member, with garlic, onions, and other alliums; John Amery with soybeans;

The next generation, Nathan Goc, Friendship, Wisconsin

Barbara Bond and her herbs; Jim Henry and his carrots. We also got to know Tom Woods from the Oliver H. Kelley Farm, and John Hartman, who had begun a small seed business, J. M. Hartman and Daughters Seed Company.

Add to this mix the expertise of Keith Crotz, a historian of horticultural and agricultural literature; Dan Bussey, orchardist and cider maker; and Jeff McCormack, a pollination ecologist who started Southern Exposure Seed Exchange with his wife, Patty Wallens. SSE had rounded up a pretty good posse.

Any experienced chef will tell you the first step to culinary excellence is selecting the finest ingredients. But the real skill is in the subtle blending, the right combination, so that one flavor does not dominate the others. Kent and I realized we could never have done this alone. Our talent—and our good luck—was in finding the perfect blend of friends, family, supporters, and associates. These people have remained in the life of Seed Savers Exchange ever since.

When I think back on those days, I'm reminded of Emerson's words: "Ideas must work through the brains and the arms of good and brave men, or they are no better than dreams." Kent and I knew that with hard work, dedication, and focus, it was possible to turn dreams into reality, and during those early gatherings at the 4-H camp, we began to identify a group to assist SSE with brains and arms.

The Youngest Gardener

Even though at times we wondered if anyone out there really cared about our mission, we were never alone in our effort to save seeds; there were many silent partners around the country—gardeners who felt as we did about growing things. Surely Glenn Drowns qualified as the youngest of this group when he took up gardening at age two and a half.

Glenn grew up in the northern mountains of Idaho near the small town of Lenore. In 1978, while doing a research project for his high school government class on current world issues, he was sidetracked by a tiny ad in the back of a magazine explaining the Seed Savers Exchange (never underestimate the power of a small ad). "The ad said something about sending $3 to get the latest seed directory," he recalls. "My family was poor, and even $3 was more than I could spare at the time. I saved extra change from selling eggs and vegetables to be able to send for the catalog in 1979."

Glenn started writing to Seed Savers in the early 1980s. Decades later, SSE has a letter we received from this young gardener, dated July 8, 1981:

My interest in gardening started when I was about 2½. I helped my mom plant a package of mixed flower seeds and expanded each year. When I was 4, I had nearly a 500-square-foot garden that I took care of myself. By the time I was 7, I really started getting interested in squash and took over the whole family garden, including ordering seeds when I was 8. I never really saved my own seed until I started seeing varieties disappear from seed catalogs about 1975. I purchased a copy of a reprint of Burpee's 1888 catalog and saw all of the varieties that were no longer available. I then began to save more seeds. I really can't say for sure what sparked my interest. I guess it was just something I was meant to do. One thing I guess that helped was being an only child and we never lived where there was anyone else my age. It gave me something to do. My parents helped me along once I got started. My father was always bringing me any old seeds that people didn't want. When I was 9 he built me a small greenhouse and I sold bedding plants every year up until we moved. . . .

I can remember when I first received the old reprint of Burpee's seed catalog how upset I was thinking about all that was lost. I searched through all the information hoping to find a source. You can't believe the number of seed catalogs I would send for, hoping that just one might have one of those varieties. Then I read about your group when I was doing a research paper in high school, and it was just like a miracle. . . .

I have around 50 varieties of squash, about 10 of which are no longer available in seed catalogs. I will probably save seed from all that I can as the way the seed catalogs are changing really scares me. . . . Some of the vegetables that I have which are still commercially available I fear are going to be dropped soon as only 1 or 2 catalogs carry them anymore. My favorite squash is Sweetmeat and I have only found it in Harris Seeds and Tillinghast, and occasionally I see a packet at the stores. Other varieties like Green and Golden Delicious are just not seen that much anymore. I also think that old-fashioned Straightneck and Crookneck aren't going to be available much longer. When I got Twilley's seed catalog this spring I was shocked to find page after page of new hybrids replacing the old standbys. Why can't people be satisfied with what they have without always wanting something better? I think that in a few years some people are going to wish they hadn't been so hasty in destroying part of our heritage.

Glenn graduated from high school in 1979 and had his first listing in the *1980 Seed Savers Yearbook*. He admitted his seed collecting rapidly grew out of control once he received the publication and had access to so much of the material he had been looking for. To make matters worse, he moved to a part of the state known as the "Banana Belt" that was warmer and more favorable to growing. He attended Lewis-Clark State College in Lewiston, Idaho, from 1981 through 1984. As of June 1, 1983, Glenn's seed collection included 227 squash varieties, 58 of watermelons, 95 of corn, 87 of beans, 48 of tomatoes, and a lot of miscellaneous.

After graduating in May 1984 with a double major in biology and natural sciences comprehensive teaching, Glenn was trying to figure out what to do with his life. SSE needed help with organizing and growing out our seed collection. Kent and I knew that Iowa had the climate and soil to produce bountiful corn crops, and we encouraged Glenn to apply for teaching jobs near Decorah. As Glenn likes to say today, "I was lured to the promised land of Iowa, where it always rains and there is rich soil everywhere. Both things didn't seem possible or natural to a native Idahoan."

Kent and I were pleased to have Glenn join the effort and looked forward to his move to Iowa in the summer of 1984. He stayed with us in our rented house until he found a very strange second-floor apartment a few blocks away. The back stairs going up to the entrance seemed to spiral through tree branches. One day Glenn opened the cupboards in his living room and found a tree trunk instead of shelves. Apparently the owner had built the apartment around an oak tree.

Most days Glenn worked with Kent at our house organizing the SSE collection. He also spent many summer afternoons in the basement of my sister's farmhouse, about ten miles east of us, where the bean cases were stored. While sorting the beans, he identified about 500 varieties that needed to be regrown.

Glenn arrived at our house with 1,000 different seed varieties; his personal interest was squash and he had collected over 370 diverse varieties. The summer of 1984 was the first year in twenty that he did not plant a garden, and he was eager to see his squash collection growing again. It became obvious that the next summer we should look for a garden spot together.

Across the fence from the 4-H camp where we'd held our campout was a narrow field with beautiful black river-bottom soil. It appeared to be the perfect location for a preservation garden.

Oxheart carrots

A Five-Acre Garden

Early in the spring of 1985, Kent and I went over to visit the owners of the field, Herb and Orabel Ehrie, to check on renting the property. We drove into their well-kept Norwegian farmyard, where colorful chickens perched on a pile of oak logs next to a Wood-Mizer bandsaw. When I got out of the car to walk to the house, I was attacked by a large white turkey. Herb said, "Oh, that was Cliff, I got him from my brother-in-law, he was supposed to be a tame one, but can be kinda ornery, loves to chase people. That turkey weighs forty-nine pounds, you know." I felt lucky to have escaped with my life. The land was available to rent and had been farmed without synthetic chemicals since 1979. SSE rented five acres.

Kent ordered a semi truckload of composted turkey manure, and Herb and his brother Jim used their manure spreaders to broadcast the fertilizer on the garden. Lorado Adelmann arrived on his tractor, pulling a mighty tiller called the Howard Rotavator, and got to work. That evening after supper we drove out to admire the fresh-tilled field. We sat on the grass of a gentle hill under a dead oak tree, watching a bluebird start to make a nest in a hollow branch. The air smelled of freshly turned earth. Before long, we took off our shoes and walked—we practically waded—in the soft, cool Iowa earth. Compared to our heavy Missouri clay, it felt like Swans Down cake flour.

Our next step was to rent bench space to start all the seedlings. Steve Elwood from the Decorah Greenhouse provided a space and offered to sell SSE the material at cost. One early April weekend, with the help of David and Gail Lange, Iowa SSE members, our small crew planted close to sixty flats of plants, including about 300 varieties of tomatoes and 100 peppers. I began to have that recurring homesteading out-of-control feeling, but I knew there was no stopping.

As soon as Glenn had arrived in Decorah the previous summer, he'd begun applying for high school science teaching positions. Openings were scarce, but at the end of the summer, Glenn was pleased to have found a job in Calamus, Iowa, about three hours away—close enough to commute to our house each weekend for planning and planting. By early June, he was back for the summer and ready to work full time for SSE. Luckily he was able to house-sit in our neighborhood for George Melby, the science teacher in Decorah, who left town each summer with his family.

The SSE garden was planted with 500 varieties of beans, 280 of

tomatoes, 100 of peppers, 50 of lettuce, 50 of peas, 120 of corn, 130 of potatoes, 120 of muskmelons, 115 of watermelons, 370 of squashes, and a small patch of Miscellaneous, like my "coffee can" asparagus seed. A few years earlier, a gentleman had sent me a three-pound Folgers coffee can full of seed. He said the plants were always grown from seed and rivaled any commercial variety, but they came to me with no name. His claim was true. These plants were eventually transplanted to a patch in front of the barn at Heritage Farm and twenty years later have developed into a magnificent bed. One good thing about growing older: your asparagus patch gets better.

Aerial view of the five-acre garden outside Decorah

Glenn standing in the middle of wilting squash vines in the 4-H garden

Each Sunday evening, after planting all weekend, we would routinely have rains. There is nothing more satisfying than watching a gentle rain soak into a newly planted garden. That continued for a few weeks. However, just as we thought, "Oh yes, this is Iowa gardening," we entered the driest summer in seventy-five years.

Aaron, who was by then twelve, helped out, using a seven-horsepower Troy-Bilt tiller to work up the ground for planting and then tilling between the rows. He was determined to keep the weeds under control, and he succeeded. But not without tiller scars.

Aaron proudly remembers how he would transport the tiller from the barn across the road to the garden: "That baby really cooks if you put it in neutral." This was good until the tiller suddenly dropped into gear and its tines grabbed the ground. Aaron, still trotting along behind, didn't stop as fast as the tiller did, and got a good-sized gash on the knee as a result. In spite of this battle wound, when the campout came around on July 20, the entire five-acre garden was weed-free.

We had heard that Pioneer Hi-Bred in Des Moines had been financing local 4-H clubs and various small garden projects in Iowa. Kent called up someone we knew at the company and explained SSE's Preservation Garden project. About two weeks later a check for $2,000 arrived in the mail.

Seed Savers still stretched every penny. Indelible markers and recycled wooden lath from an old farmhouse were used to make two thousand plant markers. Dan Zook, an Amish friend, owned a sawmill about twenty miles away near Harmony, Minnesota, and cut three hundred oak stakes sharpened at one end. We pounded them into the ground, ran strands of strong wire between them, and dropped twine strings down every eighteen inches for the pole beans to climb. Peppers grew under tents of a new, gauzy material called Reemay that covered half-bent circles of steel-grade telegraph wire. Roger Lintecum, a friend from Kansas, gave SSE the wire. Even with many hours of volunteer labor, the garden still ended up costing about double the amount Seed Savers received.

By mid-July, Iowa was in a full-blown drought cycle. The squash vines and the gardeners were both experiencing a meltdown. Growing up, I often heard my father say, "Where there's a will, there's a way." I never really knew what he was talking about until I was older.

What we had was the worst drought in seventy-five years, a five-acre garden filled with rare plants, and no irrigation system. But a river flowed just below the field. We certainly had the will, now we just needed a way to pump water from the river to the garden. The plan was that Aaron would dig trenches, using the potato plow behind the Troy-Bilt. SSE would rent a water pump and borrow old canvas hose from the Decorah Fire Department to get the water up the bank. But despite our efforts, the pump was not strong enough to fill all the trenches. We were able to water about a half-acre of beans, peppers, and most of the tomatoes.

Glenn hand-pollinated all the cucurbits (squash, melons, and cucumbers) and corn. He went out in the evening to tape blossoms and again in the early morning to pollinate. Normally he would do this only to the first few fruits on each plant. But in a drought, the plants may abort those pollinated blossoms. Glenn battled back for two months, and in the end was successful with about 85 percent of the cucurbits.

Every gardening season has problems, and with a five-acre garden we inevitably had more. Glenn says he'll always remember his experience with snapping turtles, which liked to lay their eggs in the dirt between the garden rows. One day, while Glenn was preparing to cool off in the river, Kent told him to freeze and back up if he wanted his feet. He was about to step on a big snapping turtle's back, thinking it was a rock. Another time, a great blue heron flew overhead and fertilized a ten-foot strip of the row next to him with foul-smelling material. Glenn watched the sky very closely after that.

And then there were seed-saving crises. We picked tomatoes and squeezed them, pulp and all, into quart plastic deli tubs. After a few days, a thick layer of mold formed on the top of the pulp. We took the tomatoes to the farm of Herb's daughter, Marie, to clean the seeds, holding the strainer under the hydrant on the horse tank. The green slime on the tank, combined with the fermenting mold on the tomatoes, is a scent that stays with you forever.

Still, during one of the worst droughts in Iowa history, two men and a boy succeeded in harvesting seed from about 90 percent of everything grown. Glenn says he was "energized by failure." The drought did not break till mid-August, when the frequent downpours after months of dry weather created a lot of split tomatoes. But that meant a good supply of tomatoes for preserving and for well-stocked canning shelves.

One September night Kent and I were listening to the 10 o'clock news when the weatherman announced that temperatures might get down to 25 degrees in the low-lying valleys of northeast Iowa. We both had the same thought: the peppers! In the light of the car's headlights, we picked with frozen fingers till 1:30 a.m., pulling up pepper plants, root and all, and stuffing them and their variety labels into brown paper grocery sacks. The next day we hung the plants in the shed, where most of the fruits continued to ripen.

Before the first frost that year, our family had many picnics under the oak tree and marveled at what we had nurtured. The successful seed harvest wasn't our only inspiration. For years we had known about the dangers associated with the loss of genetic diversity, but it's hard to comprehend the idea in the abstract. Walking through a seed savers' garden and seeing the diversity first-hand—the sizes, shapes, forms, and colors—makes the magnitude of what's at stake vividly real.

Early morning fog on the garden

I was able to see a Triamble squash, an extremely rare Australian three-lobed gray-green fruit, first grown in America in 1932; it reminded me of a brain. I saw a Whangaparoa Crown, a Hopi cushaw, and more than three hundred other squash. I touched a dinosaur gourd and a

devil's claw. Our family also enjoyed eating familiar produce we had grown in Missouri, like Grandpa Admire's lettuce, Amish cantaloupe, Moon and Stars watermelon, and German Pink tomatoes. We wanted to put a sign by the road inviting people to please stop and let us show them our genetic diversity—or, even better, taste it.

A quote from the Senegalese environmentalist Baba Dioum has always made sense to me: "In the end, we will conserve only what we love, we will love only what we understand, we will understand only what we are taught." This five-acre Preservation Garden above the banks of the Upper Iowa River provided the finest living classroom imaginable. There was no doubt that we had discovered an essential tool for teaching, which reinforced our dream of finding the perfect farm.

The Home Office

Soon after our decision to move from Missouri to Iowa, we began searching for a house to rent in Decorah. Only two seemed suitable: one on Main Street, next to Nordic Speedway; the other a cute yellow bungalow on Rural Avenue owned by Ed and Flo Klosterboer, who had temporarily moved to Dubuque. The Klosterboers were using part of the house for storage, but after some negotiations agreed to rent us a third bedroom and part of the basement. They made our transition to town life pleasurable—and spared us from having to listen to stock car races on Saturday night.

Living in town with our children was so convenient that it seemed like the finest vacation I'd been on for years. Our furniture even looked new in a different setting. While we would have preferred an office somewhere other than in our house, Seed Savers couldn't afford that: we set up the SSE office in the basement.

In Missouri, Seed Savers had had two employees besides Kent and me—Della Stockman and Christine Michael. The office was our living room, and on nice days Della and Kent worked on the deck. Della has fond memories of reading tomato descriptions to Kent while they were compiling the first *Garden Seed Inventory*. We enjoyed each other's company and shared coffee and baked goods fresh from my oven in the afternoon. I still have Christine's recipe for delicious buttermilk brownies with cocoa buttermilk frosting.

New in Decorah and eager to meet the locals, we attended the Oneota Food Co-op potluck, held the first Friday of each month at the Good Shepherd Lutheran Church. At one gathering, Kent struck up a conversation with Lorado Adelmann and mentioned that he was having trouble keeping up with correspondence. Lorado said, "If you ever need help, Arllys would be a good one."

Arllys Adelmann—intelligent, amiable, talented—was definitely overqualified for the SSE position; she had a bachelor's degree in secretarial science (later called business administration) from Westmar College in western Iowa. Kent proposed paying her $6.50 an hour. Arllys, who'd moved to Decorah from Minneapolis, had been thinking a bit more. Kent said he would like to accommodate her, but if he went much higher, she would make more than he did. Of course there were no benefits; we didn't even have group health insurance until 1986. Luckily for us, she agreed to take the job. In the fall of 1984, she went from transcribing medical health records and dictation for the Decorah Mental Health Center to entering the vegetable listings of three hundred Seed Savers members.

Members of the Oneota Food Co-op, which still thrives in Decorah, led wholesome lives. Arllys and Lorado were inspired by the famous homesteaders Helen and Scott Nearing. The Nearings' book *Living the Good Life* had been our inspiration as homesteaders, and I worried that co-op members expected us, as the founders of Seed Savers, to share in their earthy lifestyle. At the very least, the Whealy family ought to eat vegetables morning, noon, and night!

As a former vegetarian, hippie, yoga-practicing homesteader who now helped run a nonprofit organization dedicated to saving seeds, I was no stranger to alternative lifestyles. I certainly was not opposed to healthy living. But in 1984, our four children favored white bread bought in the store, sometimes even in the package with red, blue, and yellow polka dots. I felt compelled to hide the bread in the cupboard each morning before Arllys came to work, and limited the time the kids spent watching TV or insisted that the volume be turned low.

Arllys and I recently met for lunch and revisited those days of working in the Whealy house. "I loved it," she told me. "It was always fun around the house with the kids. You were comfortable with me being there, and that made me comfortable, too."

She recalled that Tracy and Carrie made her birthday cards. "I remember one birthday we all went to Mabe's"—a popular pizza restaurant—"and the little girls ended up fighting over who got to sit by the birthday girl," she said. "I would be included in their birthday parties or at least have cake. I enjoyed my contacts with the family and then watching the kids grow up over the years."

Arllys and Kent did the bulk mailings from our kitchen table, and she recalled having the yearbooks "sorted by ZIP code in piles all over your living room floor. Tracy and Carrie wanted to help. I remember

Arllys and Kent in the first office at 203 Rural Avenue, Decorah, Iowa

your parents would lend a hand, and the SSE extended staff family would also be called in to assist. Sometimes it seemed very chaotic when everyone was there in the living room, but we would have been elbow to elbow in the basement."

Seed Savers could not afford its own phone line, so we always shared our private home phone. I tried to answer the phone quickly during the children's naps, and we had to be careful not to tie up the line. (My children especially resented that fact as they got older.) Arllys laughed as she remembered the day Steve Demuth, our computer technician, called and asked for Kent. "I didn't recognize his voice and told him I was sorry but Kent was on the other line. Steve said, 'Don't give me that baloney; I know you only have one line.'"

Steve had volunteered to do our computer work (SSE didn't fit into any canned software program, so he custom-programmed all our software needs). Arllys says she entered the computer age with reluctance. "I was old enough that when office computers first came on the scene, I thought maybe the technology wouldn't become so wide-spread before I retired and I'd be able to squeak by without having to deal with it. I was *so* wrong. And of course I came to appreciate and rely on computers, both at work and at home. It was soon apparent how important they were to the work Seed Savers was trying to do.

"A major leap for me was when we started using the computer's capacity to sort and spew out material (address labels, curator lists, yearbook listings, inventories, etc.). I was impressed with the possibilities. And over time, as we moved up to better computers and programs, they made a big difference. Also, the addition of good office employees like Joanne Thuente and Beth Rotto meant I had help trying to keep everything running smoothly."

And it wasn't easy keeping the Seed Savers Exchange office running smoothly, especially given the number of times it moved. Less than three years after we arrived in Decorah, we found Heritage Farm, but our family and office moved four times during those first years, and Arllys always helped us with the transitions. When we finally found Heritage Farm, at 3076 North Winn Road, Arllys says she thought, "Oh, now they've found the picture-perfect farm, and we won't be moving around. It will be nice to get settled in one place."

But SSE kept growing, and the office ended up moving three more times. Finally, in February 1995, Seed Savers occupied its new office complex. "I was so happy to be in a 'real' office," Arllys recalls.

Like us, she watched the organization grow and change, moving from a small number of dedicated members whose names and personalities were almost all known to us to a larger, more diverse, and, necessarily, more anonymous group. "I suspect we had more and more people who were mostly interested in SSE's mission and work, maybe not as great a proportion who actually gardened and saved seeds themselves," Arllys says. "The seed savers are still the core of the organization, I think, but we need the support of the others, too. I was impressed that Barbara Kingsolver, one of my favorite authors, was a member of Seed Savers Exchange." (Perhaps Kingsolver found inspiration for her nonfiction book, *Animal, Vegetable, Miracle*, from us.)

Arllys, whom Kent once described as "my right hand, my elbow, and my shoulder," became the Seed Savers' office manager and, after twenty years, retired in 2004. Looking back, I appreciate Arllys's tolerance. From 9 a.m. to 5 p.m., Seed Savers was the number-one priority for the whole family, and that family included anyone who was working with us. I knew Arllys would retire someday but was sad when it actually happened. She was so professional! Any publication or communication proofread by Arllys left the office in perfect form. And I miss the familiarity and warmth she added to our home and office. Over the years, I've come to understand she wouldn't have thought any less of me had I not hidden the white bread.

Family Seed, Family Recipes

Seed Savers has been fortunate to have the backing of many prominent individuals who have offered their wisdom and their financial support. But its foundation has always been the faith and generosity of ordinary gardeners—many of them women who, by design or necessity, have become the guardians of their family's heirloom seed treasures. They were, after all, the ones who turned the fruits of those seeds into nourishment.

One afternoon in 1977, after we had lived in Missouri for a couple of years, a wonderful woman from Princeton found us at our homestead, which was still very much under construction. Rarely did anyone drive out to see us, but this visitor, Chloe Lowry, appreciated our efforts to save old varieties and had come to give us the seed of a lettuce called Grandpa Admire's, named after an ancestor born in 1822. The seed had been in the Lowry family since well before the Civil War.

Grandpa Admire's is a leaf lettuce, beautifully bronze-tinged. The summer after Chloe's visit, I went out to my garden one hot July afternoon, hoping to find some lettuce for tacos. Grandpa Admire's lettuce stood tall, its leaves still juicy and sweet—living proof of how a variety can adapt when it is grown in the same location for over a hundred years. Grandpa Admire's lettuce has become a favorite of many, not only because of its good flavor but also because of the story behind it.

More than a decade later, in March 1990, I called Chloe to hear the story again. A month later she sent me a letter:

> Surely was a surprise to hear your voice on the telephone. Am sorry to delay answering sooner. So many relatives and friends of Bertha Lowry Wade have passed on. The "Grandpa Admire's" lettuce was given to me by her when she was in her 90s. She told me at that time the lettuce seed had been in the Lowry family over 100 years. Perhaps brought here in a covered wagon from Indiana.

Chloe wrote that Bertha had also given her some "onion rosettes" —probably a clustering, perennial variety like Egyptian onions— from plants that had been in the Lowry family for more than a century in the hope that Chloe would keep the variety alive. "I planted two rows in my garden," she wrote, noting that the onions were sweeter than most, and didn't sprout in storage. Chloe died six months later, in October 1990.

In January 2009, I returned to Princeton to refresh my memories. I found Route P with no problem and drove in the right direction toward our homestead house, passing an empty spot where our mailbox used to be. On the gravel road heading to the house I saw a man in brown coveralls on foot and stopped to introduce myself.

"I used to live down this road over twenty years ago—"

Grandpa Admire's
lettuce

"You're Diane Whealy. I recognized your voice. I'm Mark Covey."

Mark was still in high school when we lived in Princeton, and I was glad to know that he and his parents, Herb and Betty, were well. Mark called his mother on his cell phone, and we were soon catching up.

I had an SSE color catalog and a packet of Grandpa Admire's lettuce seed. When Betty heard Chloe's story, she also remembered the onions. "Chloe would bring the best creamed onions to our Christmas dinner at the Methodist church. They were small and I never knew how she could have kept them so sweet into December."

Last winter I contacted Chloe's nephew, Robert Kauffman, who lives in Madison, Wisconsin. Robert told me that he and his wife, Phyllis, still spend weekends at his aunt's farm near Princeton. We talked about Aunt Chloe; I mentioned the creamed onions and asked if he might know where to find the recipe. Robert called back to report that he had talked to his niece, who still makes those creamed onions.

AUNT CHLOE'S CREAMED ONIONS

4 cups small pearl onions
3 tablespoons butter
4 tablespoons flour
1 cup whole milk
Salt and pepper to taste
1 cup crushed saltine crackers
2 tablespoons melted butter

Boil the small onions till partially done. Drain and put into 2-quart baking dish.

Melt the butter in a heavy saucepan over moderate heat, and then add flour, stirring till blended. Slowly whisk in the whole milk and continue stirring for 1 minute. Add salt and pepper to taste. Pour white sauce over the onions and sprinkle the cracker crumbs on top, then drizzle the melted butter over.

Bake at 325° for 30 minutes.

He had the recipe and told me the exact procedure over the phone. He said that in spring he and Phyllis would check all the garden spots for any survivors of the "onion rosettes." I have a strong feeling there will be onions growing somewhere on Aunt Chloe's farm.

Other seed savers have shared recipes as well as seeds. In 1983, one of our early members, Lucina Cress, from Bucyrus, Ohio, sent us a pint jar of pickled miniature red, yellow, and chocolate-colored peppers stuffed with shredded cabbage. Stuffing peppers was a time-consuming process; stuffing miniature peppers would be even more so.

We took the pickled peppers to Wellington for Thanksgiving. When we opened the jar and emptied the peppers into one of Kent's grandmother's cut-glass bowls, the red, yellow, and chocolate peppers lit up the Thanksgiving table—they were colorful enough to become the centerpiece. We expected the cabbage to taste like sauerkraut and the peppers to be spicy. To everyone's surprise, each miniature pepper was a burst of flavor, a combination of peppers and cabbage sweetly pickled.

Lucina Cress's
miniature bell peppers

I was putting the Seed Savers calendar together and thought that would be a fine recipe to include with the photo of the peppers. Over the phone, Lucina gave me more information: "An elderly lady grew these peppers in Ohio and passed them on to me. The chocolate is still my favorite, always so mild and sweet and all the plants would produce early and kept coming on till frost."

Lucina had been making the stuffed peppers for more than a decade. "I think I first listed the pepper seed in the *1981 Seed Savers Exchange*. I always offered to send the recipe for stuffing and canning with the pepper seed. Each year our branch of the hospital auxiliary stuffed miniature peppers for the hospital bazaar. We canned over seven hundred jars some years and we were sold out by 11 a.m."

She told me that she was still canning the stuffed peppers. "I just finished making one hundred jars for the church bazaar. They have become a favorite of many who come back year after year, from Florida to California. This year someone bought a dozen jars!" Initially the price was 50 cents a pint. But the peppers were so popular that the price quickly rose to $4, then to $5.50. Lucina said one customer paid $10 a pint for all he could buy.

Given all the work that I knew must be involved in stuffing and canning the tiny peppers, that price seemed appropriate to me. Lucina acknowledged that the recipe, while simple, was time-consuming. "Usually there is a group of women who get together and we all do our part," she said.

LUCINA'S MINIATURE STUFFED PEPPERS

Shred cabbage fine. For each 3 quarts of cabbage, add 2½ teaspoons salt and let stand for 20 minutes.

While the cabbage is soaking, wash enough of Lucina's Miniature Bell peppers of all colors to make 15 pints. Cut a small opening on top and take out the seeds. (I always save the seed to offer in the yearbook and hope everyone else does, too!)

Squeeze the liquid off cabbage and discard.
Add to the cabbage:

    1½ teaspoons celery seed
    1½ teaspoons mustard seed
    ⅔ cup vinegar
    ⅔ cup sugar

Mix with cabbage and stuff inside the peppers. Place in jars.
Boil together:

    4 cups sugar
    4 cups white vinegar
    2 cups water

Pour over peppers in jars and seal. Process in water bath for 15 minutes.

Another Seed Savers member, Clarice Cooper, contributed an heirloom cucumber called Grandpa Edmonson's—a cream-colored, almost white cucumber that turns red-orange as it ripens but remains crisp and good in salads. "My old aunties always grew Grandpa Edmonson's cucumber. It was large but never seemed to get bitter, and was good for fresh eating or pickles," she said. "I grew it for years. I got the seed from Daddy's youngest sister, Bernice Edmonson Hickenbottom, who still grew this cucumber in Boone County, Arkansas. She said their father started growing it in 1913."

The recipe that Clarice was best known for might have been her chocolate sheet cake, which she brought to SSE's campouts for years. She and her husband, Auburn, have been dear to me ever since they attended the first campout in 1981. I met with her recently at her home in Overland Park, Kansas, and asked her how she found out about the Missouri campout.

"I was reading an article in *Mother Earth News*," she said. "The article talked about saving seed and trying to find others who might be interested, and I said, 'Auburn, read this article. This sounds like something right up our alley!'" That first year, Clarice and Auburn had to leave the campout early Saturday afternoon to pick up their son from Boy Scout camp, and Clarice said, "I cried all the way back to Kansas City." Auburn told her, "It's OK, hon, we will never leave early again, not until the party is over."

He kept his word. In 1994, Auburn's health was too poor to allow him to travel to Iowa by car, so their eldest son, Ernie, flew them in his private plane from Kansas City to an airport near Decorah. After that year, Auburn was able to ride in the car, with Clarice driving. Auburn and Clarice attended every campout together until Auburn passed away in April 1999; Clarice attended alone until 2005.

The Coopers usually came a day early to help us stuff the registration packets, and they assisted Arllys the next day with conference registration. Between campouts, Clarice and Auburn were

Clarice and
Auburn Cooper at
the 1994 campout

always ready to pitch in. "Oh, I would just be thrilled when Kent would call and ask if we could drive over for an afternoon to help send out John Withee's bean seed to be multiplied by the Growers Network," she told me. "We would all sit on the living room floor and make up small seed packages, just surrounded with all those seeds and letters.

"And oh, the drive back always felt so satisfying. I remember one night there was a full moon that lit up the countryside so brightly we almost did not need the headlights. We recalled everything that had happened in the afternoon, ate leftover cake, shared a laugh or two, and talked about seeds all the way back to Overland Park. The memory stays with me."

Unlike some in the original group who feared that SSE was getting too big and the annual gathering was losing its family feel, Clarice always welcomed everyone who attended the campout and embraced the organization's growth. "We need as many people as we can get," she said. "It takes a lot of people to keep this thing going. I don't know how many times I've heard, 'Now, tell me again what this seed-saving thing is.'"

Clarice's enthusiasm is also a sort of seed—passed on to other members who will continue to spread the word, just as Bertha Wade and Chloe Lowry passed on lettuce and onions and Lucina Cress passed on multicolored peppers and a festive recipe.

Clarice said she didn't take seeds home from that first campout, which she and Auburn attended mostly to meet like-minded people. "I did get a start of tansy that Mary Razor had brought from Iowa. We grew it at our old house and when I moved, I borrowed a start of

Mary's tansy. It grows outside my apartment today." Although Clarice gardens in pots these days, she says her favorite tomato, Cherokee Purple, does well in containers. "And there will always be a tub for Grandpa Edmonson's cucumber."

Looking for Paradise

At the first SSE campout in Decorah, one of the speakers was Tom Woods, then site manager at a living-history farm in Minnesota. "If you tell children about plowing with oxen, they will forget tomorrow," he said. "But if they plow behind a team of oxen, they will remember for a lifetime." The same can be said about genetic diversity: You can hear about it endlessly and it may remain an abstract concept, but seeing and actually tasting the difference will stay with you, just like the taste of that juicy tomato from your grandparents' garden!

Seed Savers Exchange needed a permanent home, one where we could not only maintain genetic heritage, but also inspire others to join in the effort. A farm could be a classroom; the seed collection could be propagated in gardens; we could have an orchard and maybe even raise rare breeds of animals.

Kent and I began the search and developed a list of criteria that boiled down to *Wanted: Paradise*. The response to our initial newspaper ad, with its wish list of features, was minimal. Finally we realized that no one thought they owned a piece of paradise and if they did, they probably didn't want to sell it. We changed the ad to read "Wanted: 40 acres or more of land close to Decorah," and received lots of replies.

We took many drives through Winneshiek County with the plat book beside us, and attended a few farm auctions. At a small farm north of Decorah, along the Upper Iowa River, Kent said he was leery

Heritage Farm, 1987

of the river-bottom fields, and rightly so: the river has flooded almost every other year since. But the best indication that this was probably not our paradise was a sign posted in the barn: "Beware of Rattlesnakes."

After a two-and-a-half-year search we were beginning to feel we were dreaming the impossible dream. Then, in September 1986, Ray and Joanne Pritchard called to say they owned a fifty-seven-acre farm about four miles north of Decorah. The first time we drove into the yard, we knew that this was the place. Ray had at one time raised Arabian horses, and the pastures around the house were enclosed with white board fences, as were the corrals by the barn.

The large two-story white farmhouse stood in the middle of a spacious lawn, overlooking a beautiful Iowa dairy barn. Inside the house were many reminders of our homestead house in Missouri: open floor plan, lots of windows, a fireplace built from native limestone gathered from the property, a wood furnace, nice canning shelves, and a deck overlooking the valley.

The Pritchards had been trying to sell their farm for two years, having listed it at $215,000. Farms were not selling because of a depressed local economy and difficulties in obtaining financing. When we started talking to Ray and Joanne, their bottom dollar was $125,000. Soon we had reached a deal at a price of $110,000, including a small Oliver tractor.

About a year earlier, SSE had approached the CS Fund, a foundation that had been financing our genetic preservation projects for some years. Late in the summer, we'd told CS founders Maryanne Mott and Herman Warsh about our dream of a Seed Savers display farm. Though the foundation didn't fund capital ventures, its board understood the need to have land for the long-term goals of the Seed Savers Exchange; they agreed to loan the organization $110,000. The loan was a program-related investment of their endowed Warsh-Mott Legacy. The terms were simple; the loan was for ten years at 7 percent interest with prepayment privileges.

Around the end of October, the CS Fund sent Marty Teitel, its executive director, to Iowa to take a look at the property and complete the paperwork. Marty remembers having misgivings on that trip. "My core question was, are these people for real?" he recalled recently. "Can they really have an impact on the world?"

"When you showed me the neat stacks and drawers of used baby food bottles full of seeds in your garage, my heart sank," he told me, "because I didn't see how a small section of one garage in Iowa could save the world. What won me over was that the two of you seemed so entirely certain about what you were doing and, unlike so many people that I meet in the granting business, you didn't engage in hype or unsupported claims. You had reasons for everything, and you were unabashedly clear and frank about what you didn't know yet."

Marty also said he came to understand that, for biological and agricultural reasons, growing crops on rented land was too precarious. "I became a convert to the idea of SSE owning land. Luckily,

Maryanne and Herman instantly saw the rationale for helping with such a purchase."

On November 3, 1986, the final papers were signed and Seed Savers Exchange became the owner of one of the most beautiful farms in Iowa. We considered having a contest to name the farm. Kent had jokingly proposed "Tomato Preserves." But in a phone conversation, Gary Nabhan used the term "Heritage Farm." A name that seemed to fit in 1986 remains just right today.

The Avenue to Pine Spring Farm

Soon after SSE purchased Heritage Farm, our friend Max Quaas mentioned that he wanted to explore the ruins of a log cabin in the woods. We were intrigued and hiked up to find the remains of a stone foundation and fireplace. With help from the Winneshiek Historical Society, we were able to uncover the rich history of the farm.

The story begins with a trapper named James Kelly. His camp was located at the "big spring" (today it's at the north side of the pond). In 1848 he built a log cabin nearby, becoming one of the first settlers to claim land north of the Upper Iowa River. As more homesteaders arrived, Kelly complained that the new settlers disturbed his traps. He thought he would have more elbow room in Minnesota, so he sold his original claim to John Taylor, a land speculator who had come from Dubuque to explore the area in the early 1850s.

John W. Taylor was born in 1817, in Saratoga County, New York. His father, a prominent anti-slave politician, served in Congress for twenty years and was Speaker of the House of Representatives for two terms. In 1838, Taylor headed west to seek his fortune in real estate, traveling from Rockford, Illinois, to Dubuque, Iowa, where he made his home for several years. His first purchase in northeast Iowa

included the trapper's land. Over the years, Taylor continued to acquire adjoining land until he owned a total of 1,280 acres. After serving in the Civil War and attaining the rank of colonel, in 1865 he decided to return to his Iowa property and build a cluster of log cabins in
the dense forest above the spring and stream. He and his family spent
summers there and winters back east.

The land and residence became known as Pine Spring Farm. A
remarkable mile-long carriage road called the Avenue, graded smooth
and hard, led to Colonel Taylor's home. Working with a horticulturist in Decorah to find trees and plants that would survive at this latitude, the Colonel planted rows of evergreens and trees of many species

Colonel Taylor's log home,
Decorah, circa 1900

Local guests of
Colonel Taylor at
a card party, 1904

on both sides, interspersed with peonies, lilacs, and tiger lilies. He
invited Decorah merchants to card parties on the lawn and Sunday
dinners that featured produce and meat from local farms. Horses and
carriages were provided so that his guests could tour the countryside.

After the Taylor children were grown, the Colonel opened his
grounds to visitors. A chapter titled "Pleasure Resorts," from the 1882
edition of *History of Winneshiek County*, ends:

> We will close by saying that it will amply repay any one to visit
> the large and beautiful grounds of Col. J. W. Taylor, about six
> miles west of the city; where art has combined with nature to

make nature look still more varied and beautiful, and where frequent surprises greet the eye as one drives through avenues lined with evergreens, succeeded by flowers, solitary woods, bright and velvety openings in the forest, and finally reaches the cozy, unique log cabin of the proprietor, beyond which a bridle path leads down past a precipitous bluff to the bed of a beautiful stream, where are abundant springs, grassy slopes and green fields beyond.

One large area was kept uncultivated for the sake of perpetuating wildflowers and native grasses. There was also a fine park for elk. The park (now the valley behind the barn) was enclosed by an eight-foot rail fence to confine the herd.

Colonel Taylor believed strongly in the cultivation of apples, and planted an orchard exactly where the Historic Orchard is today. An item in *The Decorah Republican* on August 26, 1870, said: "Can't Raise Apples, eh? Col. John W. Taylor makes another positive argument that we can, by placing on our table a display of Duchess of Oldenburg, Sops of Wine, Autumn Strawberry, Sweet Pear—all fair enough, large enough, and luscious enough for any climate and any latitude. Those who try to raise apples and keep at it are the ones who never say apples can't be raised in Northern Iowa. Thanks to the Col. for this annual reminder of the fertility of his orchard."

Driving home early in the spring of 1993, I passed by the remains of the Avenue, and noticed something surprising: a blue street sign with a number. I later learned that all the gravel roads in Winneshiek County were to be identified because of the new 911 system. Roads would be assigned a number unless 75 percent of the landowners of adjoining property agreed on a name. SSE did not own property on the road, but our neighbor Virginia McLain did, and she favored naming the road, rather than giving it a bland number.

She didn't have time to gather all the signatures, but she filed the

Summer day at
Colonel Taylor's
homestead,
circa 1900

petition and was the first to sign it. Our daughter Jessica, then five, eagerly came with me to gather signatures; she enjoyed chatting with the neighbors and playing with their dogs. We succeeded in changing the name to "Colonel Taylor Road," confident that the Colonel would not have wanted his Avenue remembered as 300th Street.

The carriage road is overgrown now, but tiger lilies are still scattered beneath its gnarly white pines. Arborvitae, horse chestnuts, sycamores, larch, and apple and plum trees survive, still trying to be a part of what was once an entrance to paradise. On a walk one evening, I found a delicate plum tree, not the usual wild variety, tucked beside the Avenue. The tree was elderly, and only a few branches bore large red plums. As I picked and ate the sweet fruit right on the spot, I liked to think that the tree had been planted by Colonel Taylor himself. The tree could not have been one hundred years old, of course, but I felt his presence that evening, on the Avenue through the white pine woods above the big spring.

A year after Colonel Taylor died at age eighty-two, his log chalet burned to the ground when wind scattered sparks from a brush fire. The Colonel's story is little known, but those who visit Heritage Farm and hike into the pines to read about the remains of a once spectacular log chalet will learn it. Just as SSE has become the voice of many seeds, we are also the voice and caretakers of the history of Heritage Farm.

The Amish Connection

Not since our homesteading days had I expected to have a car just for household use. Our silver metallic Dodge Grand Caravan, purchased in 1987, lost that "new car" smell very quickly. Eventually I referred to it as the mini-truck. It made many trips to Menards for steel posts, rolls of wire, and orchard supplies. It got stuck quite often while carting fencing or picking up firewood down in the valley. Aaron remembers going to Prosper Lumber to get twenty-five eight-foot wooden fence posts; Alan Dahl, the owner, laughed as he helped load them, remarking that Lee Iaccoca, Chrysler's chief at the time, would be proud. It may not have been the best way to haul the posts, but it was the only way at the time.

One Saturday, in the early spring of 1988, we were returning from a day trip. After the van stopped at the house, Kent stepped out from the driver's seat, then four children leaped from the sliding side door. Kent lifted up the back door and two Amish carpenters in straw hats jumped out, then unloaded a king-size waterbed (luckily unassembled). Finally, a pregnant woman in her ninth month (me) got slowly out on the passenger side.

It was just the Whealy family returning from a trip to La Crosse, Wisconsin. There is a logical explanation for most of the cargo, but you may wonder why we had two Amish brothers, Dan and Eli Zook, crowded in the back of the vehicle.

Even though Colonel Taylor settled the property and many other families have since lived there, this farm is still known locally as the Halse place. Roger Halse, who grew up on the farm, said the original house had burned in the 1920s and was rebuilt. The next year the barn burned. He was not sure of the exact date the new barn was constructed, but written on the wallboard was "Monday, November 2, 1929—putting Up Aerial," referring to the barn's metal cupola and weather vane.

It was a beautiful barn, gray and weathered, but the Gothic-style roof needed our help. The roof rose thirty feet from the loft floor in great curved arches; the 65-by-32-foot loft was completely open, and the homemade laminated bows that supported the roof were just not strong enough. Roger Halse said the roof sank twelve inches within the first year.

There were several barns in the area with the same design; the barn at Heritage Farm is one of a few still standing, thanks to Ray Pritchard. When Ray and Joanne bought the farm in the early 1980s, the roof had sagged six feet in the center of the peak and the bows on the sides of the roof had bulged outward to compensate. Ray recognized the real danger that the roof might collapse and invested about $2,000 to temporarily halt the sagging. He brought in a crew that used steel cables and turnbuckles to pull the bows back into place. Then they jacked up the sagging bows along the peak with eleven 26-foot-tall 4 × 6 posts. A month later there was a seventeen-inch snow that would surely have collapsed the roof had he not stabilized it.

We respected this barn and felt the need to preserve its history, but weren't sure how to proceed. Over the winter SSE had been given several options from contractors, carpenters, and barn builders. But they generally involved replacing the bows, which meant that a good portion of the roof would have to be taken off. One thought that occurred to us was that the Amish still had barn raisings and put up many post-and-beam structures in the area. Our Amish friend Dan Zook owned a sawmill near Canton, Minnesota, and we asked his opinion. He came down in the fall of 1987 to get a firsthand look at the problem and said he would give it some thought over the winter months.

Early the following spring, Dan wrote that his brother Eli, who did most of the timber framing, was willing to come down with him and discuss the damaged barn bows. So we decided that Saturday to pick up Dan and Eli in Canton on our way back from La Crosse, not really much out of the way.

The three men went up in the loft and started brainstorming. Suddenly the solution became clear to Eli. They would need to build two post-and-beam structures. Each side of the loft would have six 24-foot-tall, 6 × 6 pine posts, topped with a 6 × 6 oak plate that would run the length of the barn. There would be two 45-degree angle braces near the top of each post. The post-and-beam structures would be held together with wooden pegs. Eli said that pushing all of the bows back into place would also bring the sides of the barn back into alignment; none of the bows would have to be replaced.

Soon the discussion came down to details. The lumber would come from Dan and would cost about half the price of material from the lumberyard. A neighbor could haul their crew and materials when needed. Eli said he and Dan would get $6 per hour; others on the crew would get $4.50 to $6 depending on age and skill. Eli said, "We don't own any electric tools ourselves. If there was some here at the barn, it would certainly speed things along."

When they came back up to the house, the final question was for me: Would I provide dinner, the noon meal, or should they pack their own? "How do they feel about peanut butter and jelly sandwiches?" I responded. It was decided they would bring their own dinners.

The crew arrived in late March, just before the due date of our fifth child, and provided a welcome distraction. In the beginning they had a driver, but most days they traveled the ten miles between Canton and our farm by horse and buggy. From the kitchen window, I could see the buggy, its horses unhitched and grazing in the corral. Some early mornings I watched them arrive, the black horses prancing in front of the barn, steam gusting from their nostrils.

It took six Amish carpenters two days to complete the post-and-beam structures. Then they added bracing to every second bow along the edges of the loft. The bows had once again taken their original shape; the unneeded steel cables hung in curved arcs in the middle of the loft. When the scaffolding came down, the loft was magnificent. Another Iowa barn would live on.

The next day, my view included four or five Amish carpenters on scaffolding, fearless and sometimes shoeless, shingling the steep barn roof. The day the new cedar roof was finished, I looked out to see sunshine lighting up the peak, reminding me of the gold dome on the Iowa State Capitol building. The carpenters then built red oak benches along the wall in the loft for seating, and a large red oak stage on the west end. Dan and crew finished their work on July 8, 1988, having spent six weeks of ten-hour days. It wasn't totally finished, but SSE's members could officially initiate the barn at the 1988 campout.

This initial barn restoration was financed with a $20,000 grant from the Ruth Mott Foundation, based in Flint, Michigan, and the foundation gave SSE a second grant of $20,000 to complete an educational facility. The Amish returned the following spring and installed restrooms and showers in the barn. (Until then, the garden crew used our house.) Gutters and stanchions that once served a small herd of

Amish carpenters shingling the barn roof

Jersey dairy cows were converted to work areas for garden staff to wash and process seeds. New wiring and lighting were added, and the milk house was repaired. The Amish workers also rebuilt a small granary by the barn and constructed a deck on the back of the barn with an entrance to the loft to accommodate wheelchairs.

I had become accustomed to seeing the lovely gray barn out my kitchen window, and when it came time to paint, felt a bit anxious about seeing a bright red barn. Kent and I had admired a barn on the way to Rochester that was a duller, richer shade of red. One day we stopped at the house and asked the owners what paint they'd used. They weren't sure but told us who painted the barn. We contacted the painter, a retired gentleman named Jake, who told us of another barn he had just finished painting outside of Lanesboro, Minnesota. The directions were to cross a metal bridge about five miles north of town, take an immediate left, and follow a narrow driveway. All of us Whealys, including baby Jessica, had a delightful evening adventure

Barn "anew"

on a one-lane road through the narrow valley with the Root River on one side, pastures and limestone bluffs on the other.

After about a mile, the road dead-ended in the farmyard and there was a barn, newly painted in a soft red. We knew we had found the right color, a Sherwin-Williams paint aptly called Red Barn. Jake painted the barn and his wife of fifty years painted the white trim around doors and windows. They would take short breaks together at a picnic table. During those still fall days, Jessica and I would often join them.

The barn now had new cedar shingles, but we still needed to find a cover for the top ridge of the roof to seal against the elements. Dan suggested trying to find an old-style metal ridge cap with round metal balls on the end, and Prosper Lumber, just up the road, was able to order one. The ridge cap was the finishing touch, like the icing on a very large red cake. The aerial erected in 1929 now reigns over a barn renewed for another century. The next December I wrote to Betsy

Walters, program officer of the Ruth Mott Foundation, to tell her that the barn was "like an extravagant Christmas ornament placed in the snow outside my kitchen window."

During those two summers our family and the families of Dan Zook and others formed a friendship that continues today. Even though I did not commit to making regular meals for the Amish, I did enjoy bringing something fresh-baked for their afternoon coffee. Their favorite was a hot oatmeal cake with a broiled coconut caramel topping from a church cookbook. Kent and the girls and I especially enjoyed our evening drives up to see Dan and his wife, Verna. The girls would play outdoors with the Zook children. Verna would often serve pie and coffee. One night as we walked toward the dark house, we heard a series of small explosions. Their daughter Susan was popping corn in a giant cast-iron skillet on top of the woodstove—their treat after an evening of gardening.

I had special admiration for Verna, who worked hard without any electricity and who truly embraced her life. We talked about cooking and baking, compared and shared recipes, and had the same appreciation for canning. One July, Verna included me in her order for peaches. The Amish community prearranged for peaches to be delivered to their farms from an orchard in Michigan. By the time I received the postcard from Verna letting me know my peaches had arrived, three bushels of the fruit needed immediate attention. I canned most of that night.

Our relationship with the Amish began with the sagging roof of a gray barn. The connection evolved and more projects presented themselves over the years. These carpenters have never disappointed us, and have earned great respect for their craft and work ethic not just from Kent and me but also from the Seed Savers staff and contractors who have worked at their side. As has so often happened in this story of growth, when SSE encountered a need, the ideal talent appeared.

Apple Lomen

By the fall of 1987, the Preservation Gardens had begun to take shape; Kent and I began to focus on our dream of establishing an orchard at Heritage Farm. Old-time fruit varieties, especially apples, were disappearing. The commercial markets focused on a few varieties like Red Delicious, McIntosh, and a handful of others. In 1900, the United States had 7,000 named varieties of apples. Fewer than 1,000 of those exist today, and their numbers continue to decline.

We felt an urgent need to safeguard fruit tree varieties at risk of becoming extinct. The Historic Apple Orchard would serve as a living museum to educate the public about this loss. SSE could exhibit specimens of the best cultivars from the past, as well as cultivars emerging from present-day breeding programs. Those trees would display a broad range of apples, with diverse flavors, textures, colors, shapes, sizes, seasons, and uses.

Dan Bussey, SSE's orchard advisor, commented at a 1997 campout workshop that most of the fruit in the orchard was from the 1800s, a period sometimes described as the golden age of apples. When settlers moved west, taking the actual apple trees was not practical. While some settlers carried small seedlings or cuttings of favorite trees, it was simpler to take seeds. Cider mills sold apple seeds by the pound. Settlers would take bags of them and plant out a seedling orchard on their homestead.

When the trees began to bear fruit, the settlers determined which varieties were good. If a variety was found to be exceptional, the settlers gave it their name. Even the names of varieties propagated from cuttings were sometimes lost or forgotten. So an apple taken from New York to Iowa could have been known by many different names.

SSE's collection is based on the material found in a USDA publication from 1905, *The Nomenclature of the Apple* by W. H. Ragan, who meticulously sifted through names and listed varieties from 1804 to 1904.

Today many breeders are trying to develop all-purpose apples. Homesteaders, who understood their fruit, planted different varieties for different purposes: early apples for pies and sauce, late apples for cider, drying, or overwintering.

In a recent visit with my Aunt Hermina, I asked about the orchard at Grandpa Ott's farm. She smiled and started counting on her fingers: "There were about eight apple trees around the yard. Each had its own purpose." Whitney Crab, on the west lawn, was canned whole. Greenings and Malinda, by the back garden, were for fresh eating. "Pa would store them in the oats to eat later in the winter, after they had mellowed," she said. Wealthy and Duchess, in the yard, were used for pies, jelly, and jams. And McIntosh could be used for any of those purposes (perhaps because of that, it's one of the few oldies that is still widely cultivated). After seventy years, she could recall exactly where each variety was located.

The tale of Johnny Appleseed may lead people to believe that apple trees were generally grown from seed. And to some degree they were, but probably only six or seven trees out of many thousands of seeds come back true to their parent variety. Pollinating insects that visited one apple blossom had most likely also visited other apple trees, so the seed had characteristics of both trees, good or bad.

To propagate a favored variety and keep it pure, someone had to take a cutting of that tree and graft it onto the rootstock of another tree. It's an ancient art; orchardists have been grafting trees for thousands of years. If an apple from the thirteenth century is still around, it must be a worthwhile variety; many generations have taken trouble to keep it.

David Sliwa
grafting apple trees
for the Historic
Apple Orchard

SSE's orchard needed to be upland for good circulation and on a spot large enough for expansion. The original Heritage Farm didn't have the best-suited property. But the eighty-three-acre property that adjoined the pine woods included several fertile upland meadows and more than twenty-five acres of Colonel John Taylor's magnificent white pines; it extended down to the valley floor, where a trout stream was framed by hillsides of wildflowers.

The land was owned by Duane and Eileen Bruening. Duane originally bought that parcel for a nature preserve. Kent told him about our vision of placing an apple orchard on the ridge, and said that adding the rest of the land to SSE property would ensure its preservation. Duane looked at Kent over his reading glasses with a slight smile and said he thought our idea was a fine one. After about a year of delicate negotiations, Seed Savers was able to purchase the eighty-three acres.

In February 1989, a small group spent nearly a week sitting around our kitchen table with dormant rootstocks and scion wood, making new trees for SSE's Historic Apple Orchard. Our orchard manager, David Sliwa, was there, and so were Lorado Adelmann and Lindsay Lee and his wife, Lee Zieke Lee. The Lees lived at the 4-H camp and had become perennial gardeners and friends of SSE. The grafted trees were packed in damp sphagnum moss, wrapped in plastic, put into cardboard boxes, and stored at about 55 degrees F for three weeks. This healing time allowed the grafts to begin growing together to form a callus at the grafting point. Then the trees were placed in cold storage at 35 degrees F until May, when they were planted in a nursery northeast of the barn. A year later, Lorado used SSE's new 1070 John Deere tractor to prepare holes to plant the trees in our new orchard. Aaron was responsible for the maintenance and watering that first summer.

The orchard was divided into three blocks: late, midseason, and early apples. Early varieties, like Yellow Transparent, Red Astrachan, and Duchess, made up about 15 percent of the trees; midseason apples, like Wolf River, Maiden Blush, Lady, and Sops of Wine, accounted for another 21 percent. The largest numbers of trees were late varieties—the kind a farmer would plant to keep a family supplied with apples for eating and cooking through the long Iowa winters—like York Imperial, Northern Spy, Black Gilliflower (Sheepnose), and Northwest Greening.

Dan Zook and his crew of Amish carpenters worked steadily for three weeks to build a fence around the perimeter of the approximately six-acre orchard site. We wanted the fence to enclose the orchard but not be visible, so we tucked it into the woods behind the scattered white pines and oak trees from Colonel Taylor's tenure. The carpenters also built a log gatehouse with a deck overlooking the orchard, to store supplies. Years later I was surprised that so many of Aaron's high school friends knew where the orchard was.

SSE's orchard started with 203 varieties from Phil Forsline at the National Clonal Repository at Geneva, New York, and 67 varieties from Charles Estep Sr. of Riverside, California. Charles, a member of SSE and NAFEX (North American Fruit Explorers), was an orchard hobbyist with a private collection of apples. He donated scion wood, including cuttings of Minkler Molasses and Christmas Pearmain.

We put special emphasis on collecting nineteenth-century apples that originated in the upper Midwest. When I walk in the orchard, I see Iowa Blush, Cresco, Duchess, Malinda, and Whitney Crab: apples from my childhood. They came from the ninety-year-old Lomen orchard, which we discovered about four miles southeast of Decorah, practically in our back yard.

Mary K. Northrop and Ole A. Lomen immigrated to America in 1848 from Valdres, Norway. West of their home, on an east-facing slope, are the remains of an apple orchard established by their son, Ole O. Lomen. In 1898, he planted nearly one thousand trees of one hundred varieties—so many that he got the nickname Apple Lomen. His brother, who raised fifteen different breeds of poultry, was called Chicken Lomen. Another brother raised horses and built a racetrack for them with a ball diamond placed in the middle. Most neighbors could never understand why he farmed the ridges and wasted the rich bottomland; he was called Horse Lomen.

Ole O. Lomen maintained his orchard until he died in 1923. Then his two sons, Erlin and Oscar, continued the orchard as a commercial enterprise until 1937. Apple Lomen's main fruit crops were apples and plums, but he also grew cherries, pears, strawberries, raspberries, and currants. His orchard provided about one-fourth to one-third of the family's yearly income.

In the spring of 1988, when David Sliwa, SSE's orchard manager, heard about Apple Lomen, he went out to visit. Oscar was living on the home place, though his brother Erlin had moved to town. I remember seeing Oscar on the streets of Decorah, dressed in a suit and tie, no matter what the season. He wore a classic felt small-brimmed hat with a tapered crown. It was inspirational to see him shuffling slowly down Water Street, moving no more than an inch at a time but getting where he needed to go.

David told me he walked with Oscar through the remaining orchard—just eighty-five trees. "Oscar visited each tree, knew every name by heart, and never had to check the label," he said. The trees had metal tags, long since grown into the trunks, but their names,

written in pencil, were still legible. "Even I had my doubts about a tree," David said, but when he checked, Oscar was always correct.

Oscar showed David photographs he had taken in 1926 from the top of the windmill, which was used to pump water. The photos gave a panoramic view of the orchard. David returned later with his camera when the orchard was in full bloom, hoping to recreate those shots. Oscar would not allow him to climb the rickety old windmill tower but said he could take photos from the rooftop of the house. So sixty years later, with help from the map drawn by Oscar, the photographs he took in 1926, and now the 1988 photos, we could identify the trees that remained.

Meanwhile, another friend, Dr. Kevin Sand, got involved. Kevin, the brothers' family physician, had acquired an antique apple press at an auction and was eager to try it out. He drove his pickup to the

Historic Apple Orchard in spring bloom

Lomen orchard and loaded the back with apples, then prepared to make cider with Golden Russet, Oscar's favorite, blended with Virginia Crab for tartness. Oscar said you needed that crabapple juice in all blends. Kevin pressed a gallon of the mix.

The next afternoon Kevin drove out to the farm with the cider. When no one answered a knock on the front door, he went around back, and saw Oscar through the kitchen window. It was a hot Indian summer afternoon, and Oscar was of course dressed in his suit and lace-up high dress shoes. He was sitting at the kitchen table, his head lying atop his crossed arms. Kevin knocked again and was relieved to see Oscar raise his head from the table. He was just listening to a baseball game on the radio, he told Kevin, and maybe he'd dozed off.

Kevin poured two glasses of cider, sipping his while Oscar took three or four large gulps, one after another. He wiped his mouth with the sleeve of his suit coat and sighed. "It's been thirty years since I tasted that cider," he said.

From the trees in Apple Lomen's orchard, we budded scions onto rootstock and planted forty-one trees at Heritage Farm. In 1990, David wrote about the orchard for the Seed Savers newsletter. He ended with an apt quote from C. W. Gurney, a co-founder of Gurney's Seed and Nursery Company. In 1894, urging customers not to be put off by the time that elapses between planting a sapling and harvesting ripe fruit, Gurney said: "You do not 'wait' for the fruit. Time will go just the same, whether you have planted a tree or not."

In this philosophical spirit, a vineyard of hardy grapes was planted in 1990 beside the rows of apple trees in the orchard at Heritage Farm. While the Lomen brothers were discovering chickens, horses, and apples, another young man, Elmer Swenson, was finding his life's passion. Elmer devoted fifty years of quiet, optimistic effort to growing and breeding hardy table grapes in his grandfather's vineyard. Before he passed away in 2004, Elmer selected over two hundred of his hardy grape varieties to be preserved at SSE's orchard, where his treasure lives on.

Each of the trees in the Historic Apple Orchard is valued for its own traits, but when I spot a Wealthy apple tree, I think of Aunt Hermina remembering where each tree stood in her parents' yard, Grandma Ott's apple pie, and canned Whitney crabapples. And Apple Lomen and his sons.

Seed to Seed

In 1976, I sat beside Grandpa Ott on a worn green upholstered couch. On the wall above the couch, my grandmother displayed her knick-knacks on blond wood shelves. A white fiftieth wedding anniversary plate trimmed in gold leaned against the wall in the middle of the bottom shelf. Nearby stood a porcelain Victorian lady, wearing a layered pink dress and carrying a ruffled umbrella. I was sitting below Grandma's collection of "pretty things" when I first held the tiny black seeds of Grandpa Ott's morning glory. Who else had touched them in years gone by?

Knowing that my personal involvement would, like Grandpa Ott's, come to an end one day, I felt a sense of responsibility. I knew that these seeds must not be planted near other varieties of morning glories, or the varieties would cross and the seed that resulted would no longer be pure. Without that knowledge, I could easily have been the weakest link in the chain reaching back to my ancestors. The seed I was given to pass on to my children would have been crossed, not the true seed. And there was a real possibility that these unusual blossoms—purple with a red star in the throat—would have vanished.

Unless the seeds are replanted and the stock kept true and fresh, the outstanding characteristic of the varieties will be lost to future generations of gardeners and plant breeders. Heirloom seed will remain true to variety year after year only if the plants are kept from crossing with plants of another variety. Say a bee visits a male flower on a Moon and Stars watermelon plant and subsequently pollinates the female blossom of a Georgia Rattlesnake watermelon. The seed from the melon that results will most likely produce neither Moon and Stars nor Georgia Rattlesnake melons but some mongrel variety—sort of a Rattlesnake Moon.

Some members of SSE are experienced seed savers and plant the same vegetable varieties that their great-grandparents grew, but others are new to seed saving. Without information on how to save seeds properly, well-meaning gardeners who are eager to grow heirloom varieties might put those varieties at risk of being lost due to cross-pollination. Luckily, some crops, like tomatoes and beans, are mainly self-pollinating—unlike watermelon and squash, which need to be isolated by distance or hand-pollinated to keep the seed pure, and thus may require more expertise.

Kent was aware of this early on, and in the *1976–77 True Seed Exchange* he included a two-page seed-saving guide. Most members were diligent and enthusiastic about passing on history and seed-saving information with seed they sent to other gardeners. Members who requested samples would receive plenty of seed to start the variety and sometimes a letter explaining the plant's history and everything they'd need to know about growing it. But a more expansive seed-saving guide was needed, especially for gardeners who were not directly involved with the Seed Savers Exchange.

By the mid-1980s, as awareness of seed saving grew, the need for accurate, simple instructions on saving seed became more acute. It seemed logical for SSE to publish a book on saving seed. After all, it had a list of members who had acquired a great deal of information through their own experiences.

Suzanne Ashworth from Sacramento, California, was one of

those members. Suzanne, a master gardener who had been in education her whole working life, was teaching at the University of California, Davis, and acting as a small-farm crop development consultant. She said that hardly a week went by in the spring and summer months without someone asking about seed saving: "Do turnips cross with Chinese cabbage, watercress with garden cress, red Malabar spinach with white?" Like many serious seed savers, she was frustrated by the lack of detailed information on the subject. She expected to find, somewhere within the walls of this country's libraries, a book to address the situation, but she found only bits of relevant information hidden in various obscure publications.

As Suzanne said in a recent phone conversation, "One day I just got fed up. I wanted correct information and wanted to find it in one place. I became very passionate that someone needed to take a stand on this seed-saving issue. So eventually, with encouragement from SSE and others, I decided to write *Seed to Seed*." She was certainly qualified: the book discusses 160 vegetables, and she has grown out every one of them, thoroughly researching and testing techniques for the home gardener along the way.

In the summer of 1988, Suzanne and her husband, Roger Ashworth, came to visit us in Iowa to meet others who would be working on the book project. Jessica, our fifth child, was four months old and colicky. Somehow I managed to clean the house, bake a pie, cook up a stir-fry with vegetables from my garden, gather flowers for the table and mantel, and remain sane. Meanwhile, our seven-year-old daughter Tracy entertained Suzanne and

Asian vegetables

The first edition
of *Seed to Seed* by
Suzanne Ashworth

Roger. I recently came across a card they wrote after the trip: "Dear Tracy, Thank you for showing us Heritage Farm. We are lucky to have such a tour guide. Have a very good year in school. Take care of your baby sister."

Over the next four years, many people contributed to the effort. Kent applied his editing skills, Arllys Adelmann typed all the extensive revisions, and Steve Demuth was the technical consultant. David Cavagnaro took hundreds of photographs on seed-saving techniques used in the gardens at the 4-H camp and donated all the photos to the book.

Suzanne graciously donated *Seed to Seed* to SSE to support its work, and she dedicated the book to our members. That generous donation to SSE has provided important revenue for our projects. SSE printed and reprinted the first edition and had an updated and expanded second edition published in 2002. Thousands of people have bought the book.

It's obvious from the organization's name that seed saving is the central component of SSE's mission and has guided our work on many levels. Over the years, numerous books and articles devoted to growing and cooking heirloom vegetables have helped promote our work. *Seed to Seed* has been an important publication for SSE, our members, and any gardener who has the desire to save seeds. Saving seed may not be as sexy as a beautiful garden or a tantalizing dish, but seeds are the key to it all.

A Monkey Puzzle

In 1988 SSE compiled a comprehensive sourcebook for all fruits, berries, nuts, and tropical edibles available from U.S. mail-order nurseries. This catalog of catalogs would have descriptions of the fruit varieties, zones where they could be grown, and, most important, the current source to order from.

So it was that SSE placed a "Help Wanted" ad in the Decorah newspaper that read, in part: "Please apply if you enjoy looking through seed catalogs." The ad was answered by Joanne Thuente, a young mother who had decided to return to the working world after her children started school. The job was temporary, but full time, and the job description caught her attention.

Joanne, who had grown up in the Decorah area, had driven by Heritage Farm and wondered why there were caged plants in the front gardens. (We placed screened cages over the peppers and eggplants to prevent insects from cross-pollinating the varieties.) She had also read an article in the local newspaper about the Seed Savers Exchange.

Joanne's gardening background was much the same as mine. She grew up helping her parents plant a garden for a large family, then helping with the harvest and canning. As youngsters, we both thought Gurney's seed catalog was the be-all and end-all. Once she realized what else was available, she became fascinated with the catalogs and loved poring over them.

She started work in August 1988. For a time, she and her children, Emily and Tyler, had a nightly ritual at the dinner table. One of the children would ask, "Mom, what funny fruits did you read about today?" Joanne would usually have a list—Ice Cream Bean or Jackfruit, both tropical fruits, or Monkey Puzzle, a conifer, or the Woodpecker apple.

The first edition of the *Fruit, Berry and Nut Inventory* was completed in 1989, but we weren't done with Joanne. We knew the inventories would need updating over the years, and Arllys, who had been updating the yearbook listings, had more work than she could keep up with. So Joanne joined the permanent staff.

The yearbook had started out as a newsletter—small, but adequate considering there were twelve members in 1976. We printed everyone's listings, along with their letters. By the next year we could no longer print whole letters, and we organized the members' listings by state. Then we moved to Iowa, and Steve Demuth began to work with the database. If we organized by state rather than variety, members who wanted a given bean would have to read through the whole yearbook to find the one they were looking for. It seemed more practical to organize by species, but that meant separating the seed from the member.

So members were all listed alphabetically by state in the front of the yearbook and assigned a code. Then the seed was offered by variety with the members' code for identification. If you name any member, chances are Joanne can give you the member's code. IA DR G, as an example, was Glenn Drowns. "When I would help with registration at the campouts, I always loved putting a face with the code," she says. "My husband and I attended the first Iowa campout and were amazed by the diversity of the characters. At the keynote address, we both noticed a seated gentleman with a long beard in his lap. I knew

Toka plum, introduced in 1911

this was the place for me. It felt healthy, a throwback to my hippie days."

By 1990, the SSE yearbook had grown out of control in the best way possible—too many listings. It was decided that the flowers and herbs listed by members would be offered in a separate publication called the *Flower and Herb Exchange* (FHE). Today Joanne updates both the FHE and SSE yearbooks.

Like Arllys, Joanne became part of the family. She was at SSE when we purchased our first copy machine, our first fax machine, and our first postage machine; she literally watched the SSE family grow up. Jessica was an infant when Joanne joined the team. "Diane's parents and Kent's mother would stop by the office for a visit," she recalls. "And sometimes Arllys and I would move card tables out onto the screened-in porch to mail books or brochures."

Joanne has read every North American commercial seed catalog and nursery catalog and every member yearbook listing since 1989. If anyone in the office wants an official answer to a question involving flowers, herbs, vegetables, or fruits, we find Joanne. If we need proofreading for seed packets, especially the Latin genus and species, we enlist Joanne's experienced eye.

The yearbook continues to be the main reason many members join SSE, and it is not possible to measure the value of Joanne, a talented amateur who has loved and cared for this part of the organization over the years. Luckily, the job has not ruined the pleasure she takes in browsing through seed catalogs. "I still enjoy it today," she says.

A Network of Growers

In 1981, Seed Savers Exchange set up the Growers Network because we wanted to multiply endangered collections that had been sent to

SSE and might be lost without our help. We had the Wanigan collection from John Withee and more beans from the collections of Russell Crow and Ralph Stevenson. We had Aunt Mary's Sweet Corn, which W. W. Williams of Ohio had kept pure for forty years, and Earliest Catawba Sweet Corn, which Phil Hewitt had kept pure for almost as long. We had tomatoes from the collections of Ted Telsch, the Reverend C. Frank Morrow, Ben Quisenberry, Edward Lowden, and Gleckler's Seedsmen; squashes from the collection of Tom Knoche and Glenn Drowns; and much, much more.

The idea was that growers could help SSE multiply the endangered collections, return some seed to the organization, and still have seed to offer in the yearbook. We also hoped that the Growers' Network could offer aid to gardeners who were no longer able to maintain a variety. I remember that we would sometimes send seed to elderly gardeners so they could still participate as listed members.

The yearbook included an application form, asking for members' growing experience, climate, and areas of interest. There was no charge for the seed; all we requested was that the growers return about two hundred seeds, or more if the supply was good. We began building up an impressive inventory of heirloom vegetables.

Skilled growers sent in boxes of their harvest every year. One I particularly looked forward to came from Russ Godard, a member in Oregon who has since died. Russ loved the Wanigan beans and took pride in the seeds he returned. The boxes contained colorful beans cleaned perfectly and still glowing from his care.

By the late 1980s SSE had over 5,000 varieties: 1,663 beans, 1,484 tomatoes, 304 peppers, 400 squashes, 158 melons, 79 eggplants, and many others. As the core collection and the Growers' Network became larger, the process was harder to control. Seed Savers had always stressed the need to keep seed pure, and we provided seed-saving guides, but we had to rely on the expertise of the grower. The risk of losing the genetic purity of the seed was too great to rely entirely on unvetted gardeners.

In 1988, the Growers Network became a Curators Network, a committed group of members who, along with the staff at Heritage Farm, would take on the responsibility of maintaining varieties in their field of expertise. The curators would renew their own seed stock and participate in the annual winter yearbook as listed members. In addition, they agreed to send fresh seed back to Heritage Farm's seed bank.

Heritage Farm would curate tomatoes, beans, peppers, and some other crops. Glenn Drowns would be responsible for corn, melons, and squashes; Suzanne Ashworth would take eggplants. Peas, biennials, and potatoes would be curated by Will Bonsall of Maine, who had been doing his own seed preservation projects long before he heard of Seed Savers Exchange. Since 1982, he has listed 4,570 varieties of seeds in SSE's yearbooks.

Will Bonsall gathering radish seed

Will's focus on self-reliance went beyond producing his own food. He wanted to close the circle and save his own seed as well. But he knew he couldn't save just the seed of annual crops like beans and tomatoes, which are mainly self-pollinating. "I also needed to learn to save the seeds that no one else thought of saving: the kohlrabi, the leeks, the parsnips," he told me. "They were more challenging, especially in Maine."

He was also interested in plant species particularly suitable for the vegan life. That meant beans, peas, and grains, of course, especially little-known grains like hull-less oats and barley, and oilseeds like sunflowers and hull-less pumpkins. "The more ignored a crop species was, the more I seemed drawn

to it, which is probably how I happened to accumulate a world-class collection of Jerusalem artichokes," he said. "It's easier to be a really big frog if you pick a really small pond."

On December 10 and 11, 1988, we held a preliminary meeting of SSE's Curators at Heritage Farm. Will Bonsall and Molly Thorkildsen took the train from Farmington, Maine, to La Crosse, and stayed with us for five days. At that time they were making every effort to live a self-reliant vegan life, and I was concerned about our non-vegan meals. They said they'd bring whole grains and whatever they could safely pack. I assured them that I welcomed the opportunity to be more creative and was ready for the challenge. The first night, we had a vegetarian tomato sauce that I had canned with ingredients from my garden. I'd purchased whole wheat pasta from the local co-op, and served lots of fresh carrot sticks and home-canned green beans.

Will took one bite of the pasta and started groaning, "Oh, this is so good, did you use oil in the sauce?" "Yes, I sautéed the onions and garlic in vegetable oil before I added the tomatoes." He sighed and said, "I can tell. It is so different when you use oil, ours without is more like tomato stew." I always think of Will when I'm sautéing the onions and garlic for my spaghetti sauce.

Will started each day at the kitchen table eating a portion of oatmeal so large he used Kent's grandmother's crockery bread bowl for his serving. He ended his day sitting by the fireplace in the living room playing his guitar. Molly would sit with one of the girls by her side, mesmerized by her knitting needles as she made scarves for them. Molly also took advantage of electricity and my blender to make almond milk, a treat that my daughters still remember.

Sour Cherries and Black Tomatoes

One July afternoon in 1990, as I was picking sour cherries, a phone call came that changed our lives and the life of Seed Savers Exchange. I was in the back yard of our friends Kevin and Leslie Sand, with a bucket nearly full of tangy bright red Montmorency cherries, when Les and I saw Kent walking fast toward the small orchard. His smile exploded with excitement as he said, "I just received a telephone call from a fellow named Ken Hope from the MacArthur Foundation in Chicago."

When I heard the word "MacArthur," my stomach took a leap. Kent went on, "The gentleman started by identifying himself from the John D. and Catherine T. MacArthur Foundation, and announcing that he had the pleasant job of informing me I had been awarded a MacArthur Fellowship."

Kent said he thought it was a prank call from a friend until the caller told him that Gary Nabhan had also received a fellowship but could not be located. Gary's associates had said that he was in a remote cave in the desert of southern Arizona, counting bighorn sheep for a survey. "I knew then he was legitimate," Kent said. "Our friends do have active imaginations, but none that creative." We stood by the cherry trees, hugging each other. I can't remember if I stayed to fill my bucket.

No one can apply for a MacArthur Fellowship—the award that the media call the "Genius Grant." Candidates are nominated anonymously by people selected by the foundation. The awards are given to individuals, not to institutions. We would receive $275,000, paid in annual installments over five years, and health insurance for the family. There were no forms to fill out, and no conditions. The check would be made out to Kent Whealy, not to the Seed Savers Exchange. In the past, all our efforts in fund-raising were for the organization. Now we had the biggest gift that anyone could have given us, and we would never know whom to thank.

Later that evening, Kent and I sat on the deck of our house, reveling in the good news. We were too gloriously shocked to even think beyond what had just happened. We had money to pay all our bills, help Aaron go to college, and buy a safe car (a member had once sent money for new tires for our car; he worried that we had no budget for that sort of thing). It wasn't hard to list all the things we had put off buying because we had no money.

Of course we both knew this award was not for creature comforts. Although nominees are evaluated for their accomplishments, the award is an investment in the future. The real benefactor was the Seed Savers Exchange. Sometimes, as Kent and I pursued our mission, we had to wonder if to outsiders saving seeds seemed unimportant. This national recognition validated our work. The publicity surrounding the award brought attention to projects that might otherwise have received little notice. It wasn't so much what the money represented; it was what the money could do.

For some people, such a fellowship would be an opportunity to pursue dreams that might have been beyond their reach before. But Kent and I could not imagine leaving Seed Savers Exchange. We were doing what we wanted to do, and we had not accomplished all that we could. We felt the award should produce something tangible for SSE and for Kent, something we could say was a direct result of receiving the fellowship. These people were gambling on us to make an even greater contribution to the world.

So we decided we would keep the focus on our work. Aaron enrolled at Luther College, we bought a Honda Accord, and for the first time we felt financially secure. The other decision we made was to forego our minimal salaries from SSE for a while. We thought subsidizing the finances of SSE would remove some financial burden from it, and some responsibility from us.

As so often happens, an opportunity presented itself at the right time. In the early winter of 1991, Kent was asked to be one of forty delegates representing nationwide constituencies and a few smaller local groups from the United States to attend the first Joint US-USSR NGO Conference. The conference was to be held in Moscow. There

Seed Savers 1991 Summer Edition

Judith Ann Griffith's vision of St. Basil's Cathedral

had been previous Soviet/American environmental conferences, but this was different because all of the participants were NGOs (nongovernmental organizations). The conference was mainly financed by the American Environmental Protection Agency, which paid for the US delegates' plane fares.

A lot of our American heirloom seed originated in the homelands of immigrants, and the diversity that still existed there was significant. One of the reasons Kent wanted to travel to the Soviet Union

Early-season vegetables from the Eastern European collection

was to find out what heritage seeds, called "endemic seeds" in Russia, were still intact. But in the past, Kent would have thought he shouldn't leave work. Though he loved to travel, he took trips only for speaking engagements. We had five children, ranging in age from four to eighteen. I couldn't easily leave the kids, but for Kent to travel to Russia seemed logical. He knew exactly what he wanted to do, and now had the freedom to do it. I would stay with the children, hold down the home front, and take care of SSE.

Kent went to Russia armed with a slide show and a suitcase of seeds, and that trip sparked Seed Savers International. This special project helped a network of seed collectors rescue traditional food crops. Many of the traditional varieties in isolated regions were rapidly disappearing because of Western agricultural technology, the introduction of new hybrids, a lack of funds to maintain existing seed banks, and, in many areas, sporadic violence.

From 1993 to 1997, Seed Savers Exchange and Seed Savers International, with help from the Wallace Genetic Foundation, provided funding for fourteen collecting expeditions. SSE financed scientists from the Vavilov Institute in St. Petersburg and Gatersleben in eastern Germany to gather seed from remote villages. We collected in Poland, Romania, Russia, Ukraine, Azerbaijan, Uzbekistan, Kazakhstan, Siberia, and Sardinia. Half of the seed was kept in its native country's seed bank and the other half was sent to SSE. In those four years, nearly 4,000 traditional varieties from thirty different countries entered the collection at Heritage Farm.

Kent got the travel bug, dazzled by the diversity that still existed.

Within two years, he made three trips to the Soviet Union and two trips to eastern Europe. In August 1991, he was invited by the Latvian ministry of agriculture to teach sustainable agricultural techniques to private farmers. On the morning of August 19, I was awakened by a phone call from Kent's younger brother, Keith. He sounded keyed up. Had I heard the news? Was Kent all right?

Not quite awake, I was sure there had been a plane crash. But Keith said there had been a coup in the Soviet Union. Gorbachev was no longer in power, the airports had been shut down, and a state of emergency had been declared. Later that afternoon, I heard from Irene Frantzen, whose husband, Tom, was traveling with Kent. She had contacted the State Department and learned that their plane had landed in Tallinn, the capital of Estonia. Knowing they were safe was some comfort, but when and how they would return remained a question. Fortunately, the coup was short-lived. It ended two days after it began.

Some people wonder whether the MacArthur fellowships are successful in their goal. I know Kent's life's work became richer because of this opportunity. If the money was intended to give creative individuals the freedom to accomplish their goals, the foundation got its money's worth. More than 4,000 vegetables and grains were saved from possible—even probable—extinction. And just when American gardeners thought they'd seen everything there was to grow, here came a black Russian tomato.

Growing Pains

SSE's accounting needs in Missouri were simple. We had a staff of two and a budget barely over $200. But someone still had to pay the bills.

I had experience writing checks to pay the family bills but had a hard time even remembering to take the checkbook when I went to town, relying instead on the local grocery store's counter checks. In those days, merchants kept blank checks from the local bank on the counter, and customers filled in the date, the payee's name, and the amount. Mastering the art of counter checks may not seem like a stellar résumé for the accountant position at SSE, but I got the job.

Fortunately, because the budget was small, the learning curve wasn't steep. My bookkeeping skills improved over the years, and I met each financial challenge. By the time we moved to Iowa, I was responsible for bills, payroll, and taxes.

Today SSE uses time sheets, but back then employees sometimes handed me small pieces of paper, torn from a tablet, with their hours noted. If I was outside the house, workers in the garden would yell their hours to me from the bottom of the hill. The Amish carpenters gave me a page from a receipt book, with the date and hours worked written neatly in pencil. Our "generally accepted accounting principles" were minimal at best and certainly we had no computer software to help. I paid all bills and paychecks the old-fashioned way, writing out the checks by hand after consulting the Federal and State Employers Tax Guide books and a calculator.

We hired a Decorah accounting firm, Hagen & Kallevang, to file all the necessary paperwork—the quarterly 941 form for employers, the 990 form for nonprofits, the 1099 forms for contract workers—but I did most everything else to save on accounting expenses. I coded the canceled checks each month with the appropriate expense categories, handled the deposits, and balanced the checkbook, making sure to call the bank to ensure transfers from savings to the checking account.

I was responsible for paying state withholding taxes to Des Moines, and the federal withholding and FICA payments had to be at the bank before the fifteenth each month. The bank supplied me with a blue zippered vinyl bag to hold the required federal and state tax coupon books, and I cared for it as attentively as I did my children. I was determined never to be late in paying those taxes.

One year, a tax due date and my due date coincided. But before Jessica Lee Whealy was born on April 5, 1988, I made sure the federal and FICA taxes had been sent in. As it turned out, for an older mom with a child who suffered from inconsolable fits of colic, a call from the IRS was the least of my problems.

By 1992, our accounting needs had grown exponentially, along with our staff and projects, and our human resource department was still just me. In October, the SSE board had voted to begin a capital campaign for $485,000 to construct a new office and seed-storage complex. (At that time, the SSE board numbered five: Kent and I, Gary Nabhan, Jeff McCormack, and David Cavagnaro.) With that goal in mind, we began considering where to build the complex.

A beautiful piece of land adjoined the north side of the property and overlooked the valley. Until two years earlier, our neighbors Bob and Judy Kvammen had lived there. But in the spring of 1990, a fire destroyed the Kvammens' house, leaving only the foundation and garage. They poured a cement slab by their driveway and moved into a camper, temporary accommodations for the summer while they built a new house. But as winter approached, construction hadn't started, and we wondered if there had been a change of plans.

Kent and I had talked often about how lovely that spot would be for the office complex if the Kvammens ever decided to move. But I didn't want to appear insensitive, and decided to wait till the appropriate time to let them know of SSE's interest in purchasing the property. In August, a young man appeared on the deck of our house and introduced himself as Dave Schmidt, our new neighbor. "My wife, Karen, is going to work for the Soil and Conservation Service in Decorah," he said. "Yesterday we stopped at Dave Kelly's realty office to check on available properties. Your neighbor Bob Kvammen had just listed his property. We went out to look at it and bought it the same day."

Bob and Judy had already left town, heading west to Oregon, before we had a chance to talk. Usually my Midwest tentativeness stands me in good stead, but in this case maybe not so much. Judy later sent me a Christmas letter: "Things happened so fast we didn't have time to even say goodbye. We are doing OK in Oregon. I just received the 1991 harvest edition and want to read it cover to cover. I really miss my ruby-throated hummers; the Rufus hummers are all I get."

Dave and Karen built a new ranch home on the foundation of the Kvammen house and became wonderful neighbors. And we chose another location for the SSE office complex. The blueprints were drawn, but we had not yet broken ground.

In the fall of 1993, the phone rang early one morning. I answered and heard Dave Schmidt's voice. "Karen and I have some news. We're moving. Karen has decided to leave her job in town, and I've accepted a job in Rochester. We just wanted SSE to know and give you first chance to purchase, before we listed the property on the market. We were thinking if you and Kent wanted to come over this evening we could talk about the possibilities."

That evening we joined them for apple pie and began negotiations. The property had an established road, water, and electricity, a metal shed, a view of the valley, thirty acres of land enrolled in the Federal Conservation Reserve Program, and ten acres of one of the best stands of white oak in the county. The other advantage was space for growth.

Maryanne Mott visited soon afterwards, and we filled her in on the available land. She knew immediately that this property made sense and agreed once again to lend the money to make it happen. The SSE board agreed as well.

Also in the works was a $125,000 grant proposal to the Kresge Foundation. The Missouri Botanical Garden had received a Kresge grant, and Kent and I had traveled to meet the grant writer in their development department. SSE submitted the grant proposal, budget, and blueprints. We felt encouraged, because the Kresge Foundation seemed interested enough to assign a program officer to shepherd the process.

We had the property, the money to purchase it, and a good chance at a Kresge grant to help toward the capital campaign. I was sleeping really well until Kent came home for lunch one day and said: "The Kresge Foundation requires an audited financial statement." SSE had always submitted financial statements with grants, but never an audited one. My life flashed in front of me. All I could think about was my nonprofessional accounting skills.

The CPA at our accounting firm would be conducting the audit, not the IRS, but I still worried about my inefficiencies. I remembered a time when my mother was coming to see us in Missouri and my house was a mess. I dreamed that I vacuumed the lawn in preparation for her visit.

SSE passed the audit and kept our nonprofit status. The Kresge grant came through and the office complex was finished. I continued to do all of SSE's accounting as it escalated over the years, with countless bills for the construction projects, managing grant contracts, Amish carpenters, and an ever-growing staff. I can almost say I never made a mistake in all those years, and I was late with the taxes only once: the check really was lost in the mail.

In 1994 SSE hired its first accountant, Kathy Hoffsommer, and invested in Peachtree Accounting software. And I've never lost another minute of sleep to accounting worries since.

Jelly melon and horned lizard

Some Assembly Required

SSE's new office, dedicated in 1995, ended up costing $600,000. Members came through by donating or pledging $300,000 in only eighteen months; the Wallace Genetic Foundation, CS Fund, and the Sol Goldman Charitable Trust, in addition to the Kresge Foundation, offered strong support.

Most of the SSE staff members had worked in our home over the years, and were more like family than employees, so we planned our office complex together. No one wanted the office to have an institutional feel; we were a grass-roots organization and felt most productive in a natural setting. In the first-floor office area, we all wanted windows that opened so we could enjoy fresh air, and they were positioned so that we could see the view even when sitting at our desks.

We ended up with seven offices and workstations, accommodating everyone's wish for either an open space or enclosed office. I hoped for a large kitchen; I always did my best work at the kitchen table. Arllys, Joanne, and I thought a screened-in porch to do mailings would be pleasant. We didn't get the porch, but an Amish-built kitchen table sits next to the door that opens on a wrap-around cedar deck.

By the early '90s, the seed collection exceeded 15,000 vegetable varieties. Until we built the new office, SSE's garden crew cleaned and processed seed in the unheated barn, where we also stored seed in the bean cases moved from Missouri. The rest of the seed was kept in basements and freezers throughout Winneshiek County. We very much needed storage facilities. The basement in the new building would contain winter offices for staff members who worked in the garden and provide adequate seed-processing areas. There would be humidity-controlled drying rooms, two large cool-storage seed vaults, a potato tissue culture lab, a mailroom, and room for storing books and products. For the first time in many years, SSE's staff and seed collection would be in one building.

Seed Savers had other needs to address as well. The garden staff had outgrown the rented bench space in the Decorah greenhouse, and an on-site greenhouse seemed essential. SSE had no suitable root cellar to overwinter our biennials (we lowered broccoli plants into the old cistern, pulling up the tall stalks the next spring to plant in the garden). A new root cellar would be built into the hill to the north of the office. Stairs inside the front entrance would lead to an underground walk-in freezer, six feet high and lined with metal shelves. Thousands of small heat-sealed foil packets of seed would be stored there. Each variety in the collection kept in the office basement would be backed up in this seed bank, disaster insurance in case a tornado or fire damaged the main building.

SSE staff on office beams, 1994

As we looked to the future, we also kept our eyes on the past. Kent and I were fascinated with barns and took pleasure in paging through books by Eric Sloane and *Barns of the Genesee Country*. Kent had accompanied Eli Zook to an Amish barn-raising near Harmony, Minnesota. The sight of heavy oak posts and beams held together with pegs in intricate joinery was memorable, he said, like the skeleton of a cathedral.

As a farm-raised child, I was comfortable in a barn. I had memories of climbing on bales in the hayloft, stacked so high we could touch the posts and beams. My brother and I pretended we were tightrope walkers, tiptoeing across the beam (of course there were bales just below to cushion us if we fell).

Everyone on staff agreed that the new office should have an Amish-built post-and-beam frame, a vanishing building technique. We all liked the idea of displaying Seed Savers' spirit of preservation. Kent contacted the Zook brothers to build our new office. In 1993, Dan cut the white oak logs for the frame. They were piled to dry at his sawmill over the winter. In the spring of 1994, the Amish crew, the logs, and a special planer Eli made to use on the logs arrived at the metal shed on SSE's new property. It took about six weeks to plane the beams and do all the notching with chisels and wooden mallets.

Kent and I found ourselves spending time in the metal shed, feeling content about the progress. One Sunday afternoon, we were joined by special guests, Wendell and Tanya Berry. Wendell was our keynote speaker at the SSE campout and we were showing them around the farm. The four of us sat on newly planed logs and shared thoughts about the art of farming, framing a building, and the simplicity of the Amish tool belt. The faint smell of tobacco from the Amish men's pipes mixed with the tang of fresh oak. Amid piles of sawdust and golden curls of wood, we anointed the office timbers with our good spirits.

The mass of logs, pegs, and mortise-and-tenon joinery was perplexing; I couldn't imagine how they would all fit together. Eli assured me he knew every single bent lying on the ground, though he did mention having his fair share of bad dreams the night before a raising. On August 9, 1994, there was an office raising at Heritage Farm. As Kent and I walked up the hill that morning, I saw the bents laid out flat on the ground and thought, "Some assembly required!"

Kent with Wendell Berry

It took eleven Amish men about seven hours to pull together the five bents and secure them with six hundred hand-carved oak pegs. Once the frame was erected, it was time for the general contractor, Stan Finholt, to begin the process of blending the simple with the modern conveniences that an office required. Steve Demuth did a masterful job of shepherding this combination. The office was a successful coordination of the talents of the Amish crew with the general contractor and various subcontractors. For about six months, two worlds came together with respect for each other's work—never a conflict, all deadlines met with plenty of goodwill and good humor. Rick Juergens, the foreman for Finholt Construction, said, "I always envied the Amish lunches. The homemade baked stuff, home-canned sausages, and fruit made my bologna sandwich look pretty pathetic."

Sometimes the Amish workers would spend the night at the office (midweek they would bunk out with sleeping bags). The Finholt crew liked to joke that if anyone drove by on the North Winn Road after dark they would see the office perched on the hillside, every light

Completed Seed Savers Exchange office, May 1995

ablaze, looking like a high-rise. They referred to the construction site as the "Amish Hilton."

At the dedication, on May 6, 1995, Kent and I reflected on the organization's humble beginnings—an oak rolltop desk in our living room—and its journey to this office complex twenty years later. It seemed inconceivable that the new office would not accommodate all of our needs. But we were wrong.

Gardens Below Sea Level

In late August 1999, Kent and I traveled to England to visit Alan and Jackie Gear at the Henry Doubleday Research Association, a wonderful group dedicated to promoting organic growing. HDRA, now known as Garden Organic, has remained at the forefront of the organic horticulture movement for fifty years and continues to be a good friend to Seed Savers Exchange.

We then flew to the Netherlands to visit the trial gardens of Kees and Elisabeth Sahin, friends who owned a seed company and were enthusiastic collectors. We stayed at the Golden Lion, a lovely hotel in the small village of Sint Annaland (population 3,500) in the province of Zeeland. We walked into the hotel, where several older gentlemen sat around wooden tables drinking glasses of beer and playing cards. A man behind an ornate carved walnut bar greeted us and handed Kent the key to our room.

Eager to see the gardens before sunset, we followed a road atop the dikes that led to Stavenisse. The road overlooked paved bike paths on either side; local women in dresses and men in straw hats held hoes at their side while pedaling back to town from the fields. Wicker baskets on their handlebars overflowed with gardening tools, cabbages, and flowers. We drove by fields of nasturtiums, sunflowers, and acres of cosmos and zinnias being harvested for seed with large combines. We passed by fields of night-scented tobacco, and as the perfume flooded the car I felt like Dorothy, intoxicated by the poppy patch on the way to the Emerald City. After a lifetime of living beside fields of corn and hay, this truly seemed like the yellow brick road.

Kees and Elisabeth had established their flower company in 1982 with varieties collected and bred by Kees. In an effort to increase diversification in the seed trade, their company planted trial gardens at Zeeland each spring with thousands of different flowers from around the world. On a single day, Sahin gardening staff sowed the seed of more than 8,000 strains of annuals and perennials directly into the ground; apart from weeding, the plants required no care and thrived under the Dutch sun.

While the gardens were close to the sea, they were below sea level. We drove down a dirt path and as soon as I stepped out of the car, I

Sahin trial gardens
in the Netherlands

was struck by the silence. It was both weird and wonderful to see the tops of silver windmills peeking over the dike. Cowbells rang on the leather collars of a small herd of Jerseys grazing above us, on the green slopes of the dike that held back the sea.

I began to feel lightheaded and very peaceful, as if I had overdosed on charm. The damp sea air mixed with the fragrance of sweet peas, the rows of tall bright yellow sunflowers set off by a clear blue sky—we seemed to be in a painting by van Gogh rather than a garden plot.

After watching the sunset from the gardens, we returned to the village and went to a restaurant across the street from our hotel. While our Dutch was not the best, Kent recognized wiener schnitzel from his travels to Germany, and I noticed that the fish of the day was snapper, caught that morning and served on a bed of sea kale, a vegetable that has fascinated me since I read it was grown in Thomas Jefferson's garden. We also had a fresh shrimp cocktail in a wide clear glass goblet. The shrimp, in a delightful tomato sauce, were so tiny we ate them with spoons. It was our introduction to a delicacy the locals called sea beans. "They taste like the ocean!" I exclaimed.

We sat on the terrace with a bottle of wine and watched villagers out walking or riding bicycles on the narrow streets and paths. Occasionally we would hear voices in the distance or the turning of bike wheels. Older ladies rode back to their rural homes, their baskets filled with bread, flowers, and whatever else they needed from the village. Our favorite sight was a group of young boys riding down to the marina with bamboo fishing poles, their faces alight with excitement.

Kees and Elisabeth arrived during the night and left a message to meet them for breakfast. I walked into what had been the bar the night before, to find it transformed into a banquet room. The long tables were covered with colorful cloths and set with white china. Down the middle of each table were large plates of sausages, hard cheeses, breads, and hard-boiled brown eggs. I will always remember the aroma of fresh-brewed coffee, very strong and served with cream so thick I needed a spoon to put some in my cup.

As we chatted with Kees, the owner of the hotel handed us a message: we needed to call the SSE office. My heart started to race. I hardly ever left the children home alone and now I was out of the country! But the kids were fine. Instead, the message concerned a proposed visit from Martha Stewart. She was attending the Iowa State Fair and, since she was so close to Seed Savers, wanted to film a segment or two for her TV show. Her visit would be just three days after our return from Europe. We knew this was a great opportunity for SSE and of course gave the go-ahead for the shoot.

In Zeeland, meanwhile, we spent the whole day with Kees walking through the garden. I knew he could be irritated with visitors who hadn't done their homework; he'd expressed disappointment that seed companies often sent buyers who were not gardeners. Kees not only had amassed a large horticultural library but also had read every book and seemed to remember all he had read. So many plants had disappeared, he said, that you needed to know what had been grown before if you were to recognize something unique when you saw it.

I followed Kees in the garden and hoped that my honest enthusiasm would disguise the fact that I knew the common but not the Latin names of each variety. It was dazzling to see so many old-fashioned annual flowers I had read about, visualized, and hoped still existed; we took notes and photographed varieties that SSE members might want.

Kees was known for large grow-outs, once growing 5,500 kinds of pansies just to find the truly black one. He trialed 13,000 violas to select a mixture he called Historic Pansies; it closely resembled those grown in gardens in the 1800s. There were about 850 varieties of marigolds, including some that grew to my waist. We saw old-fashioned forget-me-nots, four o'clocks, salvias, and verbenas four feet tall, as well as single moss roses, tassel flower, cleome, and "bees' friend"—Bienen-Freund in German—a lovely annual with lavender-blue flowers much coveted by bees.

A woman from Ohio had once sent me a package of Bienen-Freund, with a letter saying that she was from Germany and had grown it in her garden there. She brought the seed back from a trip because she wanted her daughter to see bees working in the garden. I was thrilled to actually see a whole patch and, yes, it was swarming with bees.

At one point in the afternoon, Kees picked a handful of what looked like green snails. He had a mischievous look in his eye and a mysterious grin, and said, "Open your hand, here's a handful of caterpillars." Of course, I reluctantly obeyed. I opened my hand and exclaimed: "What are these little hairy things?" "*Scorpiurus muricatus*," he replied, "native to southern Europe, and once offered by Vilmorin in the late 1800s."

I was sure he expected me to understand, but before I could react, he laughed and said, "Prickly Caterpillar. I have the entire collection. In days past, these 'caterpillars' were added to salads to surprise diners. Not many seed companies bothered to maintain them. The tight pods are narrow and twisted like a caterpillar rolled upon itself, and the seed is very hard to extract."

I had a handful of riches. The caterpillars were carefully packed with the rest of my souvenirs. Over time they have turned a brown golden color, but I still have them proudly displayed in a dish above my kitchen sink with other precious finds from my travels. They will

Prickly Caterpillar

always bring a smile as I remember Kees and Elisabeth and our visit to the Netherlands. The plants can also be found in the display garden each year at Heritage Farm; they have lovely pink blossoms that turn into caterpillars.

That day with Kees, I sniffed every sweet pea, tasted white strawberries, and watched a local family harvest the biggest cabbages I had ever seen. The next day Kent and I drove to Alphen aan den Rijn to meet back up with Kees. After checking into our room at the Hotel Thor, we decided to take a drive to Gouda and spent the afternoon tasting cheese and gazing at the architecture, which looked like a continuous row of decorated gingerbread houses surrounding the town square.

When we returned to the hotel, the phone was blinking with a message. It was from Kees, inviting us to accompany him to the flower-buying market in Amsterdam at 3 a.m. Our flight was leaving early that morning, so we couldn't go. It was my only regret on the trip—

even more so because Kees passed away in September 2006. There are still gardens in Zeeland, but no one there to hand you, with a playful grin, a vegetable caterpillar. Elisabeth decided to sell the company to a Japanese firm and remains active as a consultant.

Martha Stewart Is in the House

Kent and I arrived back in Iowa late Monday evening. We were jet-lagged and had only three days to get the gardens and grounds into perfect shape. After being gone for a week, leaving teenagers in charge of a ten-year-old and pets, I was not concerned about the condition of the house, just grateful it was still standing. As I expected, housekeeping projects had been slightly neglected.

Because Martha Stewart was scheduled to film in the display gardens and grounds at Heritage Farm, we focused on the outside. It was a once-in-a-lifetime opportunity to promote SSE nationally, and we needed to look our finest. The itinerary called for Martha to take a short flight from Des Moines to the Decorah airport, while the camera and sound crew drove vans for the three-hour trip. We expected her to arrive around 8 a.m. But because Des Moines was fogged in, her flight was delayed about two hours. I was pulling a few last weeds from the display garden beside the barn while we waited for her to arrive. I looked up to the house when I heard the sound of cars and saw three vans pulling into our drive. The vans parked in the drive beside the house instead of the parking lot at the garden as we'd expected. The sound and audio crew were getting out of the van and so was Martha Stewart. Kent and I hurried up the hill together and I thought: Please, let's get to her before she goes into the house, which was of course a mess.

Luckily she saw us and started walking toward the barn, not the house. We reached the vans somewhat out of breath but able to welcome her to Seed Savers. We shook hands, and she was so cordial and down-to-earth that Kent and I immediately felt comfortable. She had done her homework and knew about gardening and cooking with heirloom vegetables. She also knew about SSE, asked thoughtful questions, and seemed fascinated by our work.

She mentioned that because of the fog delay, she had not had a chance to put on her makeup, change clothes, and get ready for the filming. "Would there be a place where I can set up shop?" she asked. "Even the garage would work."

Kent and I looked at each other and silently agreed that was not a possibility. Anyone who knew about the Whealy garage knew we hadn't been able to park our car inside it for years. One side was filled with empty milk jugs, accumulated in case of a late spring frost. The jugs could be used to cover many hundreds of pepper and tomato plants (and they were put to work one Memorial Day weekend). The old informational kiosk was stored in the middle, and the rest of the space was filled with gardening supplies, tractor tires, and pretty much everything else that needed a roof for storage.

I said, "Oh, I don't think that would work out, our garage is kind of a mess."

"Really, all I need is an extension cord and a place to sit down."

Kent and I both said at the same time, "Please come in the house."

She replied, "OK, I can just use your kitchen table."

Again Kent and I looked at each other. We'd been up before 6, gulped coffee, and rushed outside. Totally ignoring the kitchen, I made sure the display garden was in tip-top shape, the small visitor center/gift shop in the barn stocked and in order. We helped the garden crew pick apples from the orchard for Martha to taste. We picked tomatoes and had everything we would need to demonstrate tomato seed saving. Everything was in perfect order . . . except my kitchen. As we walked toward the house, I said under my breath to Kent, "Stall her in the parking lot."

We'd made sure the lawn had been mowed, which meant a lot of grass tracked into the kitchen. With grass clippings on the floor, dirty dishes in the sink and on the counter, two daughters still sleeping on the floor in the living room, and Martha Stewart heading for my house, I was focused.

In the living room, I told the sleeping girls, "Wake up, get your blankets picked up, Martha Stewart is coming in the house to put her makeup on." They were a bit dazed but recognized the panic in my voice and knew they had to move quickly. Jess, who had gotten up with us, excited to meet Martha, found a broom and started to sweep up the wet grass. I stashed dirty dishes in the oven, then grabbed a laundry basket from the utility room and swept everything off the kitchen table (along with any other clutter within my reach) into it. Then I crammed the basket inside a closet.

I heard voices as Kent opened the back door into the kitchen. Martha entered carrying an armful of clothes she would need to change into and a white pastry box. "Come in. Sorry for my messy kitchen," I said. "I have five children and have been out of town." It was my standard excuse. Martha said, "Oh, please don't worry. It looks just like mine." I thought, right, I am sure you have dirty dishes in your oven.

The box was filled with chocolate brownie muffins, a new recipe for us to try. I was pleased that she noticed my Watt pottery above the kitchen sink. It was the apple pattern; the creamer came from the Festina creamery and the sugar bowl from Huber's Store in Fort Atkinson, and they were my favorite pieces. Her appreciation of them put me at ease.

Soon Martha was set up at the kitchen table with everything she needed, a light with a mirror and the young woman who was going to put on her makeup. I went back outside, but the girls were happy to stay inside and visit. They watched her get ready for the show. At one point, Martha said to Tracy, "Would your mom have any coffee made? I'd love a cup."

Tracy looked at the counter and saw that some coffee was left in the bottom of the pot from the morning. "Would you like cream or milk?" she asked, and Martha replied, "Cream would be great." In the refrigerator, Tracy found an old carton of half and half, poured some into the coffee, and thought to herself, "Good, it didn't curdle." They all chatted for about an hour, a great experience for my daughters and one they will always remember.

After Martha came into the gardens, we filmed two segments in less than four hours—one in the orchard, followed by an

Martha Stewart often mentions the SSE catalog on her shows

apple tasting of varieties from the historic trees, the second a walk through the Heritage Farm display gardens by the barn. There she filmed us talking about SSE history and current projects, and we demonstrated the process of saving tomato seeds. I was glad we had devoted so much time to the garden. She was impressed with the burgundy okra, and as we stood beside the row, we shared okra recipes.

Mine, I told her, was from Kent's mother. "Just cut the okra in quarter-inch pieces, dip in egg and milk, put cornmeal in a large brown paper grocery sack, add okra, shake, remove, and fry in hot oil." Martha said, "That sounds like the traditional Southern recipe for fried okra. Another one of my favorites is to sauté onion and garlic in olive oil, add okra and chopped fresh seeded tomatoes." I tried the recipe, and it was a great way to disguise the sliminess factor of okra (and no doubt more healthful than fried).

After the filming, everyone piled into one of the vans to give her a whirlwind tour of the office, seed collection, and storage facilities. The last stop was the Robert Becker Memorial Library, upstairs from the office. Martha was drawn to a worn brown copy of *American Horticulture from 1873*, the title embossed in gold. We all relaxed sitting on the oak benches below shelves of *The Fruits and Fruit Trees of America* and across from the whole series of *Vegetables of New York*.

"The family of the late Robert Becker donated this collection of horticultural books," I told her. "One afternoon after the books were placed on the shelves I was sitting on this bench. It struck me how the collection of seed is stored in the basement, the literature about the varieties is stored up here, and in the middle are the folks responsible for bringing the seeds to life with their stories."

We shared an admiration for the valuable horticultural information in the books, and appreciated the sense of nostalgia evoked by the rich musty smell of the worn leather covers. But we also talked about the future—potential collaborations with SSE—and felt a great sense of accomplishment for such a short visit.

Carrie had gone into Decorah and picked up sandwiches for a late lunch. Martha grabbed hers, gave everyone a hug, and headed to the La Crosse airport. The crew stayed behind to finish shooting.

Those two segments aired in October 1999, and the office phones started ringing. Each time the segment replayed, it drew the same intense interest. In 2009, Martha mentioned SSE in her episode entitled "Gardening 101," and email inquiries and requests for catalogs were off the charts. When I give lectures around the country, one of the most frequent questions is "Did Martha Stewart really visit the farm in Iowa?" I can definitely answer, "Yes, and she had coffee in my kitchen!"

The Roscoe Connection

In the mid-1990s, I spent most summer days working in the tiny gift shop in the barn below the house at Heritage Farm. SSE's staff was small, literally—Jessica, then about ten, helped me out. When I gave tours of the farm, Jess would accompany me, occasionally holding a favorite kitten or pushing a whole batch in her doll stroller. Roscoe, our black and white Border collie, was also by my side.

We had rescued our farm dog from the local vet, who had been asked to put him to sleep. Roscoe had been acquired by a farmer who intended him to herd dairy cattle, but Roscoe was afraid of cows. The trait that made him useless to the dairy farmer was a boon for us. He became the Heritage Farm mascot, an unofficial greeter who ran to cars after they parked, wagging his tail and welcoming everyone as they headed for the barn.

Roscoe, family Border collie and Heritage Farm mascot

Roscoe was also afraid of storms. The Amish carpenters had constructed a special opening in the back door of the barn so he could get inside, and I can still hear that little door clapping shut and see Roscoe running into the gift shop to hide under a bench. He was our meteorologist—he knew that a storm was approaching long before we heard the distant rumble of thunder.

One August afternoon in 1999, a man named Jamie Banks came to visit. He arrived just as I was starting a tour and asked if he could tag along. Afterward, we struck up a conversation and started talking about seeds and my four-legged sidekick. Jamie asked the dog's name, and I told him Roscoe, the name his former owner had given him.

165

Jamie laughed and said, "Gee, the only other Roscoe I know is my friend's uncle in southern Iowa. Maybe you know my friend—Greg Brown, a folk singer." I told him that Kent and I had gone to a Greg Brown concert at Luther College in 1987. I was pregnant with Jessica at the time, had four other children, and was preoccupied by the business. All I could remember of the concert was a song about canning peaches. Since then I've learned that the lyrics go like this:

Peaches on the shelf,
Potatoes in the bin,
Supper's ready, everybody come on in . . .
You can taste a little of the summer, my grandma's put it all
     in jars.

The song was "Canned Goods," Jamie said, and it was set in Greg's grandparents' farm in southeast Iowa, a part of the state that Iowans refer to as Hacklebarney. The song also refers to the farm's root cellar—now long gone. Jamie told me that Greg liked what we were doing, and was in fact the one who put him in touch with Seed Savers Exchange.

"I wonder if Greg would be willing to play a benefit concert for you at the farm," he said. "He was planning to take the next year off to garden and fish, but I could ask him. Would you be interested?" I didn't have to think long about that one. "We would be thrilled!"

Jamie and I exchanged telephone numbers and addresses and he went back home to Maple, Wisconsin, near Lake Superior. Shortly afterward, he wrote to tell me that Greg was indeed interested in doing a benefit concert at Heritage Farm and would donate all proceeds to Seed Savers.

One day late in the following spring, I heard Joanne greet a visitor in the gift shop. A low pleasant voice replied, "I'm just looking for seeds and to see if Diane is here." I walked over to see a man looking through books, wearing a tattered straw hat, sunglasses, and earrings with feathers. "Hi," he said. "I'm Greg Brown."

We toured the farm and I showed him the barn loft, where Eric Tingstad and Nancy Rumbel, recording artists from Washington State, had given benefit concerts in 1996 and 1997. To my untrained ear, the acoustics sounded good, with oak timbers and a cathedral-like ceiling. I invited Greg to stay in the Korsen cabin, which SSE used for guest housing. It

Korsen log cabin built in 1876, restored by Amish carpenters in 1993

had been built in 1876 by a Norwegian immigrant family and perfectly restored by the Amish carpenters in 1993. Its log and mortared rooms quietly recaptured the spirit of the farm's past, and guests could sit on the deck and listen to the babble of Canoe Creek. They could watch lightning bugs—or even the northern lights.

Greg seemed impressed with the operation and offered to do two concerts on consecutive days if the loft got too crowded. He wrote the name of his agent on the back of an ATM receipt and went on his way.

On August 12, 2000, Kent and I were sitting on the deck behind the barn when the concert crew arrived and joined us. Greg was wearing a vintage hot pink SSE T-shirt with the sleeves cut out; Cowboy Bob, an old friend from the '70s, was in overalls. Bob's brother, Mark Voit, and Jamie arrived carrying a cooler of beer. They had just finished roofing a barn at Greg's grandparents' farm in Hacklebarney.

We all sat on the deck overlooking the display garden in the late

Greg Brown performing in front of the asparagus patch at Heritage Farm, 2002

afternoon, enjoying a few beers and the smell of fresh-cut grass before taking Greg and his group to the Korsen cabin, already provisioned with a berry pie, scones, and a fifth of Jack Daniels.

The next day, Tom Goodmann, a friend of Greg's who teaches medieval literature at the University of Miami, joined the group. They were interested in finding South Pine Creek, after hearing it was one of the few Iowa trout streams with native brook trout or, as Tom liked to call them, "Ice Age brookies." Kent gave them directions to the creek, which was in Pleasant Township, about twenty-five miles north on meandering gravel roads. We hoped they would find their way back in time for the concert.

They did make it back somehow. No one was wearing a watch; they were just fishing away and watching the sun. The group showed up for sound check at 5 and they were a sight. They had been wearing only shorts and T-shirts, and their arms and legs were slashed from scrambling through bushes and thick beds of brambles, trying to find South Pine Creek. They were never sure they had.

The temperatures had soared into the 90s during the day, and by

Saturday evening the loft was steaming hot. This space was meant for hay bales, not people. We used a rope and pulley to ease down the barn door to let some fresh air into the loft, but it didn't do much to cool the space. "It was approximately 120 degrees up there," Greg recalls. Still, he was a trouper. He sat on a chair in the front of the loft, wearing an orange jumpsuit zipped up the front to cover his itchy, burning scratches. There was a hot light shining on his face and very little air circulation. But he didn't keel over, and he performed one of the best concerts I've ever heard.

After the concert, Greg and friends returned to the Korsen cabin. Tom Goodmann eloquently summed up the evening: "Late that night on the porch outside the old cabin, among all of these growing things—flowers, berries, nettles, vegetables, trout bred in the tank and in the stream, pretty White Park cattle, and friendships—we share the thought that this would be a good day to take leave of the earth, allowing as that day will come to us all. It has been a day that has given far more than enough . . ."

Even after we nearly roasted him in the barn, Greg was willing to give another concert the next summer. Kent and I decided to move the concert outdoors and use the hillside below our house, which creates a natural amphitheater. "I've never played in front of an asparagus bed before!" Greg said at that second concert, and he assured everyone that outdoors was a lot better.

We relied on good weather for the annual concerts, and we have been fortunate. When I was growing up on my parents' dairy farm, each day's work revolved around the weather forecast. But whatever the weather, there was something to do: gardens or field crops to be planted ahead of a rain; hay to be cut, dried, and baled in a dry spell. I remember my mother saying that during her childhood, brides who didn't want rain on their wedding days would hang a rosary in the west window—or was it on the clothesline? But I never really understood what a deal-breaker weather can be until I started organizing outdoor concerts. The one thing that can make or break the evening is the only thing completely out of your control.

The closest to disaster we came was on July 1, 2006, when a storm had the nerve to form right above us. It came out of nowhere and included hail. But by 7 the sky had cleared, the sun was shining, and Greg's daughter Pieta began the concert. Jamie Banks, Greg's long-time friend and also Pieta's godfather, said later, "Pieta's clear soulful voice was just what we needed, the perfect end to our late-afternoon storm that brought back the sunshine."

At the seventh concert, propitiously held on the seventh day of the seventh month of 2007, we discovered that seeds can become a path to salvation. That year Greg invited the Reverend Dr. Samuel Mann, from St. Mark's Episcopal Church in Kansas City, to join him at the concert. Dr. Mann, or the Reverend Sam, as we called him, was a close friend of Greg and his wife, Iris Dement (and had in fact married them). As they were driving through Iowa, it was hard not to notice cornfields, and the conversation naturally led to corn.

"It's a fine-looking crop," Greg told Dr. Mann, "but probably most of this corn is genetically modified—GMO—corn, and in some cases it is even illegal for farmers to save their own seed corn from year to year."

"That's a sin!" Reverend Sam intoned in his best preacher's voice.

Greg invited Reverend Sam to say a few words before the concert, and Reverend Sam was definitely worked up about fields of GMO corn. His message was that manipulating the genetic code of life to keep farmers and gardeners from saving seed was a sin; saving seed was the way to salvation. It was a true case of preaching to the choir, and he drew an enthusiastic round of applause. That concert was recorded live, including Reverend Sam's words, and Greg donated the recording to SSE. The CD, *Sin, Salvation, and Saving Seeds*, has thirteen tracks from the concert and original cover art painted by Greg Brown.

Greg returned to Heritage Farm on July 11, 2009, for his eighth concert. Even though the crowds grew larger, the planning never became more difficult for Jamie and me, working behind the scenes—just more entertaining. Over the years, Greg has been accompanied by his wife, Iris Dement; by his daughters Zoë, Consti, and Pieta Brown; by Bo Ramsey, Karen Savoca, Pete Heitzman, Joe Price, Dave Moore, J. T. Bates, Jon Penner, bullfrogs, and lightning bugs.

Greg has become one of our great friends, generously donating 100 percent of the concert proceeds to Seed Savers. And the concerts have brought friendship, family, and music into our lives. People from all over the country begin the evening on the lawn as strangers and leave as part of a larger family, passing along our garden heritage.

"Seeds Savers to me is a place of hope—hope that we will turn away from the doom we have manufactured," Greg told me in a recent

The lawn in front of the barn at Heritage Farm filled with folks attending the Greg Brown concert email. "That we will cherish this place, Earth, where we live, take good care of it and of each other. Seed Savers is action, not just words and ideas . . . I felt so good every time, singing, felt so full of gratitude and tomatoes I thought I might pop. It was always hard to do other shows after Seed Savers. . . . None of them were in the middle of a big garden full of nourishment and sunflowers, and the sun going down over those mysterious old hills."

Roscoe lived a long and happy life as Heritage Farm's dog. One spring day in 2002, he came up to the north side of the house, lay down in my lily of the valley patch, and died. But he had made an appearance on *Martha Stewart Living*, had letters addressed to him from fans and visitors, and was serenaded by Greg Brown. In his second concert at Heritage Farm, Greg dedicated his song "Like a Dog" to Roscoe, the farm mascot. And as Jamie pointed out, "These concerts might never have happened if Roscoe hadn't introduced us in the first place."

Cover Stories

In the early 1980s David Cavagnaro read about John Withee in *Organic Gardening* and answered the call to help John regenerate the beans in his collection. "I had an altruistic goal of looking for bean varieties that performed well in my California climate and at the same time I could help John with his grow-out," David recalls. When John gave his beans to SSE, we inherited David as a resource. It was not long before David found us in Missouri and joined SSE as one of our early Lifetime members.

On January 3, 1983, David wrote to SSE: "*The 1982 Fall Harvest Edition* is a masterpiece. I simply don't know how you do all this without going bananas. If $100 will help, then here it is." Attached to his

letter was a three-page résumé. While I was playing on the farm in Iowa and enjoying myself in Estes Park, David had spent his childhood overachieving. Since 1961, he had published more than eight hundred photographs and articles. In 1972, he was the photographer for Time-Life Books' eleven volumes on the American wilderness. His photos had been published in *Life, National Geographic, Audubon, National and International Wildlife, Sierra Club,* and *The Audubon Society Field Guide to North American Trees.* He had written and illustrated several books and was the cinematographer for wildlife sequences in the movie *Never Cry Wolf.* He taught biology and photography.

David's letter ended with typical generosity: "So, my friend, there is much to do and much to share. I hope that we may connect in person, and I am looking forward to the day when I can be of more direct

David Cavagnaro's eggplant collage taken at Heritage Farm that appeared in a full-color centerfold of *Audubon* magazine, 1989 help to you and your worthy project. Meanwhile, here is a bit of money to keep the home fires burning, and some seed to heal the world with."

Two years later, we had the opportunity to meet. Kit Anderson, from the magazine *National Gardening* (formerly *Gardens for All*), was writing an article on the 1985 campout. She would need a photographer to accompany her and had contacted David in California. That was also the first year of the Preservation Garden. *Audubon* magazine later quoted David's description of that garden: "There's a tremendous sense of history here. I'm really conscious of it when I walk through the garden. I feel like I'm walking through the history of agriculture on this continent . . . and the history of agriculture on the planet. It's esthetically important too, because a diverse world is a more attractive world."

In a more recent comment to me, David was less formal: "I about lost my mind when I saw it," he said. "I was like a kid in a candy store." After his return to California, David prepared a set of slides—more than eighty-five of them—from the campout and garden. One set went to Kit, another to SSE.

"In 1984, I had a respectable collection of seed myself," David recalls. "I was flabbergasted touring the Exchange's garden, exploding with vegetable varieties. This garden was also an astonishing introduction to the history of the world's food supply, family heirlooms from every corner of the world. It was incredible; I don't think I have been more excited anytime in my seed life. There was a selection of more than 200 tomatoes, the beauty of food that I could show through a photo. . . .

"The interest in heirlooms in the mid-'80s was beginning to take hold and the media would need photographs. I had a respectable reputation and connection to the media world as a nature photographer. I could supply the images for articles and SSE would receive the publicity." At that time, there was no money for advertising or promotion; we relied on the media to spread the word, and David already had those connections. The color photos that we could now provide with articles made our work visually appealing. David said we once calculated that between 1987 and 1995, at least one major article on SSE was published in a national magazine or newspaper every month.

Our gorgeous pepper collection appeared on the cover of the November 1989 issue of *Audubon* magazine; the credit read: "A selection of peppers from around the world, photographed at Seed Savers Exchange by David Cavagnaro." Inside, the magazine had an article titled "Heirlooms in Your Garden" with a full-color centerfold of heirloom tomatoes, eggplants, corn, and beans. Membership inquiries nearly tripled after the Audubon exposure, and grew even more when other magazines, including *Smithsonian*, requested photos and stories.

David had used a camera lens to chronicle the stories of these living heirlooms. When asked to speak over the years, I have relied on his slides to steal the show. David's images remain as captivating today

Peppers from the SSE collection, featured on the front and back cover of *Audubon* magazine, 1989

A collage of tomatoes from the SSE collection that filled the center pages of *Audubon* magazine, 1989

as they were in the early 1980s, and have been reliably wowing audiences ever since. Heirlooms have gained popularity since those days, and some of the vegetables are not that uncommon today. But I am quick to point out that the photos were taken almost twenty-five years ago. SSE was ahead of its time.

After his visit to Iowa, David made another offer. He said, "I took one look at that huge garden and could see you needed help, and gardening is something I can do. What would you think if I offered to come out and run the garden for free next summer?" We said, "Yes!" David returned to California to discuss the move back to the Midwest with his wife, Joanie. "I didn't have to do too much persuasion," he reported. "We were up for a lark."

The next spring, David drove to Decorah with every slide he

owned packed in the back of his car. He and his sixteen-year-old son, Pippin, stayed with us in the house we rented on Rural Avenue. Joanie and their daughter, Carina, flew out later to join them. They all moved into the house that Glenn Drowns had lived in the summer before.

Soon after they arrived, David had to leave for a week to teach a photography class in Maine. He recalls feeling worried about Joanie's mental well-being. She had spent much of her life in Berkeley, and would surely feel the stress of being transplanted to northeast Iowa. "When I returned," he says, "the first words out of Joanie's mouth were, 'I don't know about you, but I'm moving here. I've felt more comfortable in Decorah in one week than I have my whole life in California.'" Joanie says she remembers asking me what I did during the winter, and I responded, "I take coats on and off kids all day."

A full page of beans from the SSE collection showcased in *Audubon* magazine, 1989

Two full-color pages of SSE's collection of Indian corns published in *Audubon* magazine, 1989

David went on to be SSE's garden manager at Heritage Farm for eight years, and continued his photography, gardening, and writing in Decorah. He has served as advisor and is on the current SSE board. He has donated the collection of photos taken at Heritage Farm over the years to Seed Savers Exchange, and we rely on it for calendars, catalogs, and any other opportunity we have. The elegance of those photos is as timeless as the living plants they capture.

Thirty-six years have passed since Kent and I began our journey. I could not begin to know how many people have entered the life of the Seed Savers Exchange. The level of support ranges from simple nods of approval and appreciation of our work to people who move their families to Iowa from California. In the early years, SSE never had the financial resources to adequately compensate those who worked with us. Looking back, I realize that when there was a vacancy, a good-hearted person appeared to fill it. A belief in the cause and a desire to help guided these folks to Seed Savers Exchange.

John Swenson once likened SSE to an organism, "a force that will grow and thrive despite difficulties. Like a plant with genetic resistance to blight, insects, and disease. There may be a cosmic component and plan that drives this organism." Of those who have contributed over the years, he said, "They become one of the 'sparkles' on a gem."

David had his own take. In his first visit to the campout, he ended his speech with this observation: "You never know—as Kent with his Seed Savers Exchange would be the first to tell you—when a vision, a dream, something that you love takes hold of you, when you get there and share it with the world, you never know what these things are going to grow into. Seeds always germinate into something, sooner or later."

Seed Politics

The "amateurs" have been the guardians of our genetic resources for some thousands of years. There is no need to stop now, and they have one advantage over institutions: i.e., the true meaning of "amateur" is one who loves or cares. There is no substitute for enthusiasm.

JACK HARLAN
Professor of Plant Genetics, University of Illinois

SSE has attracted a talented group of amateurs—self-taught experts in fields as diverse as the seeds they are keeping. Just as diversity is the basis of vigor in seeds, it is the strength of our organization, and we know we must all respect each other's "seed politics" regardless of political or religious affiliations.

Winter squash

As a nonprofit organization, SSE cannot engage in political activities or adopt political affiliations. But where there is money, there is bound to be politics, and the lucrative seed trade itself is intensely political. Seeds are big business in several industries, not just agribusiness but also the food, oil, and pharmaceutical industries. As a small grassroots organization, all we could do was what we did so well: save seeds, work the gardens, and be ambassadors to other gardeners. But we were not entirely powerless against the forces of politics. Because we were amateurs—saving plants because we loved them—we had a much stronger motivation than money. And we had allies.

We had, for example, friends like Pat Roy Mooney in Canada and Cary Fowler in the United States. Not only did Pat and Cary bring a knowledgeable perspective on seed policies to our members, they also became the political voice for seed savers around the world.

Kent first met Pat around 1984 at the Seeds of Yesterday and Tomorrow conference in Toronto. Their friendship was a marriage of strong ideals with a loud and well-respected political voice, both aimed at protecting genetic resources. Pat has since been a highly effective advocate for SSE. He gave the keynote address at the 1990 campout, entitled "The Genesis of a Global Movement," which ended with this thought:

> At the end of the day, when everything has been studied and analyzed and spliced, the seed will always still be the first link in the food chain. If you control the seed, you can control the entire food chain. We have a choice. We can let a few governments and a few corporations take control of the seeds and the food system or we can let the farmers and gardeners control it. But . . . we've all got to deal with this choice together. Community seed banks, farmer-curators, and gardener-curators are going to be what keeps the world alive and keeps the seeds free for all of us to use. "Give us this day our daily bread" should not be a prayer to a government or a corporation.

We became familiar with Cary Fowler, who now serves on the board of SSE, even earlier, in the late 1970s. Cary, who was also committed to the diversity of food crops, had written a guide to sources of heirloom fruit, nut, and vegetable varieties at about the same time we were beginning the True Seed Exchange.

I recently listened to a talk Cary gave at a TED conference (TED is a small nonprofit dedicated to Ideas Worth Spreading; the letters stand for technology, entertainment, and design). All of us might have been under the influence of the late Dr. Jack Harlan, who once wrote, "These resources stand between us and catastrophic starvation on a scale we cannot imagine. In a very real sense the future of the human race rides on these materials." In his speech Cary said those words made a deep impression on him, as they had on Kent and me.

Cary has initiated grass-roots work against plant patenting by nongovernmental organizations, published dozens of articles on genetic resources, and co-authored four books. Perhaps his most lasting contribution is that, as executive director of the Global Crop Diversity

Trust, he was instrumental in winning approval of and financing for the Svalbard Global Seed Vault, a high-tech seed bank located on a Norwegian island. Svalbard is like a safety deposit box for biodiversity and global food supply preservation, storing duplicate collections of seeds from around the world. The Seed Vault offers protection against loss of diversity because of natural disasters, wars, equipment failures, accidents, and loss of financing that can plague even the best gene banks.

In 1985, Cary and Pat won the Right Livelihood Award, sometimes referred to as the "Alternative Nobel Prize," for their work in saving the world's plant genetic resources. In 1998, Pat received the Pearson Medal of Peace from Canada's Governor-General. *The Ottawa Citizen* reported on the award in an article headlined "Biodiversity 'crackpot' wins Pearson medal: Activist wages war against 'life patents.'" In the article, the Governor-General describes Pat's efforts: "He raised the alarm and created a higher public consciousness of the threats to biodiversity. His achievements show us the impact that one person can have when he cares deeply about an issue: He raised the chance for peace."

In 2001, Pat, Cary, and Hope Shand formed the ETC Group (Action Group on Erosion, Technology, and Concentration; pronounced "et cetera"). Pat's, Cary's, and Hope's passion continues today. They have fought tirelessly for decades—opposing legislation, for instance, that would have permitted big seed companies to refuse farmers the right to save their own seed. They have been the voice of reason, speaking out for the protection of our genetic resources even when few people wanted to listen. For their wisdom and perseverance, they are held in great esteem by many in SSE and elsewhere. I'm grateful that, because of their interest in our common cause, I have only needed to wage war on weeds in my garden, not on multinational conglomerates.

From Paper to Pixels

(decorative ornament)

I have in front of me a yellowed six-page document, hand-typed and hand-stapled, called the *True Seed Exchange*. In it, twenty-nine members list heirloom seeds. Also in my office is a 2011 SSE yearbook, which has five hundred pages and lists seeds from more than seven hundred members. I remember the handwritten letters from 1975. For the 2011 yearbook, many of these listings arrived electronically, via the Internet.

I would never propose going back to the past. Growth is good and the transition from Rural Route 2 to www.seedsavers.org has brought with it convenience and access to information that is timely, accessible, and readable. Still, I mourn the loss of a certain personal element. When the mail was opened, it disclosed some letters written with pristine penmanship on fine stationery, some on crazy recycled paper or even paper napkins. Letters came written in proper blue-black ink, and in crayon. Once we received an envelope addressed to "Tomatoes," Decorah, Iowa.

SSE's first communications were almost all through the mail. We had no business phone, and we didn't publicize our home phone number. Anyway, long-distance calls were expensive. Not until 1988 did Seed Savers have a separate line. Today SSE has twenty-five phone lines.

Over the years, SSE publications have been created with a typewriter and duplicated on a copy machine or mimeographed in our back bedroom. Now, with printing presses, an entire publication can be dispatched with the press of a button. At first there was just one publication, the *Seed Savers Yearbook*. In 1982, we added a *Harvest Edition*; in 1986, a *Summer Edition*. In 2009, we added a *Spring Edition* and also started to print in color.

Since 1991, SSE has published gorgeous calendars with photos from David Cavagnaro and Rosalind Creasy, a pioneer in the field of edible landscaping with a passion for photography, beautiful produce, gardens, and seed saving. Ros has been an untiring supporter of SSE since the 1980s and serves on our board of directors.

The SSE board approved publishing and mailing a product brochure in 1992. Until then, we sent out separate mailings to announce publications like *Seed to Seed*, the updated *Garden Seed Inventory*, and SSE calendars. I worked with Becky Idstrom, a staff member who had experience with Adobe PageMaker, to produce handsome small brochures offering a few products, mainly books related to gardening or seed saving.

In 1993, SSE had decided to offer heirloom seeds from Heritage Farm's collection and traditional varieties from Eastern Europe and the former Soviet Union in a leaflet that we called *Seed Savers International*. Buyers did not have to be members of SSE to purchase seeds. We felt this was an opportunity to educate nonmembers and get them involved. Once they had a pack of seeds in their hands, it would be easier for them to understand the importance of SSE and saving seeds. We succeeded in attracting new members, and the seed sales became a substantial source of income, which was then used to maintain the collection. Gardeners were happy to purchase the seed; SSE had a great way to educate the public, distribute more seed from the collection, and get the financial help the organization needed to become more self-sustaining.

In the fall of 1997, we replaced this modest black and white seed list with a color catalog. Then in 2000, the Seed Savers *Catalog of Heirloom Seeds, Books and Gifts* combined both mail-order efforts. This catalog has evolved into an informative and stunning sourcebook, and a place to showcase the work at Heritage Farm. It has become our best ambassador. Everyone, gardeners and nongardeners alike, seems drawn to the beauty of this catalog and our seed stories.

In 1999, we launched www.seed savers.org. Nothing done in the past ever equaled the publicity and success that this expansion produced. A year later, SSE offered the option of ordering online, in addition to ordering by mail, phone, or fax.

To fulfill those orders, some changes had to be made. When SSE built the new office, we planned for an order-fulfillment room in the basement with what we thought were plenty of shelves and counters. But when we added seed packages to the product inventory and SSE customers increased, we suddenly felt crowded. The phones in the office rang almost nonstop, and we ran out of space for workstations.

The basement overflowed with seed that needed proper storage. The lobby and conference room were jammed with seed, seed packets, and seed packagers. In the spring of 2008, SSE completed a new seed house, just across from the office. It's devoted entirely to mail-order operations, seed storage, and packaging. The office is once again used for seed collection, membership publications, and education.

By 2011, about 80 percent of SSE's orders come through the website and much of our communication is through email. But a real person at the other end of a telephone line is still our trademark. We can

Garlic, onion, and Rouge Vif d'Etampes pumpkin

profess efficiency in the electronic age, but there's no substitute for the human voice at the other end of a telephone line. That mode of communication will never be out of style at 563-382-5990.

A Friend Back East

While Kent and I were growing vegetables, a family, and an organization, a teenager was discovering the pleasures of gardening on the North Shore of Long Island. Amy Goldman loved to walk in the woods and in an abandoned apple orchard where big old standard trees still grew. She appreciated her mother's delicate peach tree and fragrant rose garden. It was the beginning of a lifelong passion for growing.

When the Goldmans moved to another North Shore suburb, Amy explored the land around their house and found a spooky old building that evoked gardens from the past. As she writes in one of her award-winning books:

> Off in a forgotten corner of the property was a drafty old greenhouse (minus half of its glass), a mysterious relic that no one but me cared much about—until I started producing tomato plants there. The structure stood on a rise, steps away from an abandoned garden. Later I would plant an orchard on one side and grapes on the other, reclaiming the land . . .

"As a teenager, I had a very receptive audience for my fruits and vegetables—my family adored fresh produce," she recalled recently. "Both my parents were experts in their own way, my father as a former grocery man and my mother as a fabulous cook. Her specialties were

Hungarian goulash and stuffed peppers with tomato sauce. Nothing made my father happier than the fruits of the earth."

Amy was already on a path that has led her to become one of America's most distinguished heirloom plant conservationists. She shared her love of heirlooms and efforts to find varieties that had disappeared from seed catalogs with other SSE members. She began to seek out books on gardening and seed saving, and eventually encountered the writings of Cary Fowler, Pat Mooney, and Rosalind Creasy.

Cary Fowler and Pat Mooney's 1990 book, *Shattering: Food, Politics, and the Loss of Genetic Diversity*, "made me a card-carrying seed saver, collector, and advocate," she says. And *Cooking from the Garden*, one of Rosalind Creasy's books, showcased the gardens at Heritage Farm and introduced the mission of the Seed Savers Exchange. "Ros is a luminary in edible gardening," says Amy. "She introduced me to a new world of 'rainbow' vegetables, and to the gardeners and chefs who were growing and cooking these wondrous fruits."

In 1991, Amy joined Seed Savers Exchange and in 1992 became a listed member. In addition to being an accomplished gardener, Amy was executive director of her father's foundation, the Sol Goldman Charitable Trust. The trust helped SSE complete the capital campaign for its new office complex, and she came to Iowa for the dedication. It was the beginning of a wonderful, fruitful friendship and collaboration.

Amy soon became a very active member of SSE. Like all seed savers, she carried her fascination for seeds with her wherever she traveled. In 1994, while she was studying the French language, her tutor showed her a magazine article about a pumpkin festival, where rare and forgotten vegetables would be on display. That October, Amy attended the Tranzault Pumpkin Festival in the French heartland and wrote about it in *Seed Savers 1997 Summer Edition*.

Amy obtained seed from dozens of squashes at that festival, and gave them to SSE. We decided to plant these rare squash in the gardens at Heritage Farm in 1997, in addition to the 800 varieties already in the Seed Savers collection. The squash grow-out would be an opportunity to evaluate the squash collection, checking seed duplicates, purity, and viability. When all plants were being grown under the same conditions, SSE could take data on growing habits. Varieties in need of regeneration could be hand-pollinated, and it was a grand opportunity for photographs.

One of Amy's impressive photos from the festival was of a two-wheeled oxcart spilling out a river of squash. Kent and I wanted to reconstruct that scene in front of the barn at Heritage Farm, and we had plenty of squash—but no oxcart. Kent was able to locate a back axle, a couple of wagon tongues, and two wheels of a yet-to-be-restored covered wagon. We created a mock oxcart in front of the barn, and set up the most amazing squash spill in the United States. Photos of it still appear in magazines.

In September 1997, when Amy returned to the farm for a squash viewing, she said she hoped that Kent and I would come to New York for a visit. The next summer, we took her up on that offer of a tour of New York City, and saw Central Park, the Unicorn Tapestries at the Cloisters, and much, much more.

Jessica still has the copy of *Eloise at the Plaza* she bought on that trip, and vividly remembers the day when the car door opened and a white-gloved hand reached down to her as the doorman said, "Welcome to the Plaza." We visited Katz's Deli and indulged in real pastrami. We had New York egg creams and knishes. Jessie ordered turkey with cream cheese on a bagel, and our waitress said, "No one has ordered that before—I think we'll call it a 'Jessie.'"

I asked to visit Ellis Island, and we all talked about its history as the portal of heirloom seeds. For a moment I felt a bit of the thrill my great-grandparents must have experienced, even though the Statue of Liberty hadn't yet been erected when they arrived in the United

Heritage Farm's own
squash spill, 1997

*Seed Savers
2002 Summer Edition*

Banana, Jenny Lind, Old-Time Tennessee, and D'Alger melons

States. They most likely passed through Castle Gardens at the tip of Manhattan Island, which then served as the immigration station for New York State.

The next morning, we all headed to the New York Botanical Garden for a meeting and tour given by Gregory Long, its president, who noted that he'd first learned of terminator technology from SSE. He was referring to, in Amy's words, "the trend that privatizes, monopolizes, sterilizes, and even causes seeds to kill their own embryos."

After our city adventures, we drove north to Old Sturbridge Village, where Kent was speaking, and later returned to Amy's farm and gardens, near Rhinebeck, New York. Amy invited Carolyn Male, an SSE supporter and author of *100 Heirloom Tomatoes for the American Garden*, and many others to a delightful lunch. Her table was set with potted peppers, corn, and gardening tools, and the lunch included blueberry spritzers, baby mesclun salad with raspberries, and poached salmon with cucumber and dill. Dessert was Paradise, Black Tail Mountain, and Cream of Saskatchewan watermelons.

Carrie recalls being overwhelmed by all the fresh melons. She'd been surrounded with melons most of her life, but they were grown for seed and she'd never before been able to taste so many. We sat in Amy's garden and ate plate after plate of melon. One night, Amy took us to eat at her favorite restaurant in Rhinebeck because of its CIA connection. When we looked concerned, she laughed: "Relax, it's the Culinary Institute of America." Students from the institute, not far away in Hyde Park, practiced their craft on patrons of the restaurant. Carrie was evidently inspired by her simultaneous discovery of melons and the CIA; she returned to New York and in 2005 graduated from the Culinary Institute of America. She's baking her Midwest specialties (and her mother's) for a coffee shop in California now, dreaming of owning her own little bistro.

For me, the highlight of our trip to New York was the towering compost pile in Amy's yard. The colorful melon shells made it seem as if a rainbow had fallen on the farm. Amy had obviously been under the influence of melons for quite some time. Her parents, she said, loved them. She'd won innumerable prizes for her melons and written magazine articles on them, and people began urging her to write a book. By the late 1990s, she was ready to do it, in partnership with Victor Schrager, an internationally exhibited photographer who is a frequent contributor to *Martha Stewart Living* and gardening magazines.

Kent and I were pleased to offer SSE's support to a partner who had taken such a serious interest in the Seed Savers melon collection. While the seed was maintained at Heritage Farm, SSE did not have the time or money to publicize these forgotten fruits. With Amy's expertise in gardening and her artful eye, we knew this seed would generate new interest in growing and maintaining unique varieties of heirloom melons. Aaron, who managed the SSE seed catalog, began planning with Amy to increase the seed of particular melons. We knew that gardeners who read Amy's book would be disappointed if the seeds were not available to them.

In the fall of 2000, Kent and I returned to visit Amy at her farm in Rhinebeck. We found her in the kitchen, surrounded by melons. She was hard at work, like a scientist, meticulously recording data, dissecting melons, and measuring the sweetness of their juice with

a refractometer. The next morning we read Amy's melon book proposal and were impressed with her knowledgeable writing and the
photographs that illustrated it. Collective Farm Woman, a Ukrainian
melon, was portrayed with the same elegant beauty as the Prescott
Fond Blanc cantaloupe from a French market.

We devoured melons at frequent intervals all weekend and took a
photo of some of her Hollybrook Luscious melons, which we needed
for the SSE catalog. There was a French melon called Noir des Carmes
that I wanted to take back to Iowa, so we packed a small box for the
road. On our flight home we stored the box in the overhead compart-
ment, and by the time our plane landed in Minneapolis, the whole
cabin was perfumed with Eau du Noir des Carmes.

In the fall of 2002, we made another trip back east to visit Carrie, then a full-time student at the CIA. Amy, who had accepted our
invitation to join the SSE board of directors in 2001, invited us all to
her house for dinner. Her book on melons had been successfully published and widely praised, and she'd started another project.

We arrived at her farm to see piles of squash of every size, shape,
and color imaginable on the stone walls near the house and in washtubs on the porch. And Amy was again in her kitchen, with squash
piled high on every flat surface, including the floor. There was squash
in the basement, and behind the double doors to her garage were
tables, made from boards and sawhorses, entirely covered with even
more squash.

Her squash book was published in 2004, and she didn't stop there.
In 2008, Amy's book on tomatoes became the latest expression of her
passion for growing and the fruits of her garden. I especially love the
cover, which bears a handsome photograph of two ripe German Pink
tomatoes. Each of her three books—*Melons for the Passionate Grower*,
The Compleat Squash, and *The Heirloom Tomato*—has won the American Horticultural Society's Book Award. SSE is proud to have her as
chair of our board.

Marketing Seed Diversity

In the early 1990s, the gift shop was in the corner of the red dairy barn at Heritage Farm. Visitors would pass by a bed of wispy green ferns from the asparagus, then stroll through the flower and herb garden, where they could stop and admire Grandpa Ott's morning glories climbing up twine strings that covered the entire south side of the barn. I'm sure the plants would climb over the barn roof if there were strings to latch on to. Just outside the gift shop, on the step to the barn door, are seven handprints, lined up in order of size, on a concrete step. The hands are from the Whealy family, and the date 1989 is inscribed above our one-year-old's small fingers.

The Whealy family handprints, 1989

Carrie and Tracy
Whealy modeling
the first SSE
T-shirts, 1988

As the kids have grown, I am ever more grateful for this reminder of their childhood. I have loved hearing the voices of children outside the door as they placed their hands on the various sizes and exclaimed, "This one fits!" I've been happy to identify each hand: "That was my daughter Carrie when she was seven years old. How old are you?"

A vine or two of morning glories usually tried to slip in under the door, but we never minded. Occasionally a tree frog, hidden in the morning glory foliage outside, would be visible through the window inside the shop, its little suction-cup feet attached to a pane of glass. A butterfly might flutter in through the top of the open door or a barn swallow might quickly swoop in and out. It was a small shop, filled with colorful posters, seed packets, and books; sometimes you could find a kitten curled up in a woven Tarahumara basket.

In the early 1990s, I worked most days, weekends included, with occasional assistance. My best helper was my youngest daughter, Jessica. Jess liked to count change back to customers from the gray metal money box. One day an elementary school teacher compli-

Jessica Whealy helping out in the eggplant patch during a garden tour

mented her: "I just love to hear children be able to count back change. I sure wish they still taught that in math classes. It is becoming an extinct skill."

For years we had mulled over the idea of opening an off-site non-profit retail store. SSE was already generating substantial income from its mail-order catalog and had developed a successful gift shop at Heritage Farm. Decorah was in an isolated rural area with a population of 8,000, and the farm and gift shop were open to visitors only in the summer months. A store in a larger community would increase our educational outreach while generating project-related revenue to help SSE become more self-sustaining.

The board agreed, and approved our proposal to sign a lease for a storefront in Madison, Wisconsin. On February 26, 1999, we held the grand opening of Seed Savers Garden Store. I loved this project, which satisfied my yen to manage a bona fide retail store. Whenever my travels took me to a botanical garden or museum, I liked to explore gift shops, looking for ideas. The garden store gave me space to feature such items, and I even had two store windows for displays. Aaron, who managed the Seed Savers catalog, became the store manager and lived in Madison, but I made the three-hour drive nearly every week to create new displays and help the staff during busy times.

At a meeting in March of 2002, SSE's board approved a $1.9 million capital campaign to purchase Twin Valleys, adjoining Heritage Farm. It had been nine years since the 716-acre property was bought for SSE by Maryanne Mott and Herman Warsh, who'd agreed to hold onto it until SSE could take it over. The board was concerned that the purchase might financially strain the core operation of Seed Savers Exchange and Heritage Farm. But with a major donation from Amy Goldman, the board believed it would be possible.

Part of the budget for the capital campaign included construction of a visitors' center and museum gift shop near the barn at Heritage Farm. Amy Goldman's mother, Lillian Goldman, died in the summer of 2002, before the visitors' center was completed; it was dedicated to her and bears her name.

Once again, an Amish friend and carpenter, Henry Miller, was

Each summer, thousands of visitors tour the display garden next to the barn at Heritage Farm

enlisted in design and construction. Stan Finholt, who had previously worked with these Amish carpenters on the SSE office, was general contractor. The frame of the Lillian Goldman Visitors Center, with 900 pegs, was more complex than the frame for the office, which had a mere 600. Henry placed curved diamond braces around the inside walls, and used a technique called hammer bents above the gift shop. With this technique, the beams are stepped up and over, a bit like stair steps, so the inside of the structure is completely open.

Kevin and Leslie Sand donated ninety oak logs from his late grandparents' woods near Ossian, Iowa. Kevin had planted these woods with oak, walnut, and ash trees, all from seed, and there was a fine growth of new trees in danger of being shaded out by mature oaks. The gift would give SSE three-quarters of the oak logs needed for the post-and-beam frame of the visitors' center. In March 2003, while the ground was still frozen solid, it was time to cut the trees.

Summer gardens at Heritage Farm

The Lillian Goldman Visitors Center at Heritage Farm, Decorah, Iowa

Kevin called his friend Tim Carrol, a logger from Lyle, Minnesota. Using horses, Tim did a masterful job of getting the trees out of the woods without tearing up the new tree planting. The logs were soon spread out along the drive, and once again the metal shed by the office was filled with curved braces and stacks of beams drying and awaiting assembly.

The dedication and grand opening of the Lillian Goldman Visitors Center was held on February 26, 2005. The whole board of directors, along with many from the community, watched as Amy Goldman cut a wide red ribbon with a pair of pruning shears. Each year, thousands of visitors pass through this structure, which is a work of art. Fashioned into frame and beams, those oak trees offer the same sense of welcome and comfort as they did when they supplied a canopy of strong branches and leaves in Kevin Sand's grandparents' woods.

Though the Seed Savers Garden Store in Madison had been well received, the board decided that two stores were not feasible. So we closed the Madison store and moved all its fixtures and inventory to the Lillian Goldman Visitors Center, where we could highlight our work at Heritage Farm. Not only does the new space eliminate the occasional problems of bees, snakes, and other creatures, it provides large handicapped-accessible restrooms and space to accommodate busloads of tourists.

The visitors' center also means we can host more events and involve more of the local community. In 2006 we had our first tomato-tasting event and more than 700 people attended. I could not ever have imagined attempting such an event in the older barn. And while I never met Lillian Goldman, I hope she would have been pleased to see the center that bears her name filled with a crowd in such good spirits, celebrating with plates full of beautiful and delicious tomatoes.

Jessica tagging along on a garden tour with her favorite kitten, Katie

The Twin Valleys

Twenty years earlier, in the spring of 1986, Kent attended a weekend gathering at the Land Institute in Salina, Kansas. The institute—founded in 1976 by Wes Jackson, a plant geneticist, and Dana Jackson, then his wife—works with perennial polycultures, the intermingling plantings of perennial grains. Kent decided to attend the festival to reconnect with our friends from Native Seed/SEARCH, Gary Nabhan and Karen Reichhardt, who were speaking, and to learn more about the Land Institute as a possible model for SSE's Heritage Farm.

He must have come away inspired, because later that year SSE purchased Heritage Farm. That fall, Wes was speaking in Decorah, at the Oikos Conference (Oikos is the Greek word for "house" and the root word for "ecology") at Luther College. Kent and I attended his lecture. After he finished answering the audience's questions, we kidnapped him and drove out to the farm. We ended his visit by climbing the stairs leading to the barn loft, where we sat for a bit and talked.

Wes knew the excitement we were experiencing. He and Dana were about our ages—Kent was thirty-nine and I was thirty-six— when they purchased the first acreage for what became the Land Institute. They started with a small property and eventually added more. Wes, who is known for his quick wit, said he didn't want to own much land: "just mine and all that adjoins it." After all of our dreaming, SSE had finally found fifty-seven acres of paradise. Kent and I could not imagine ever needing another acre.

Directly above our house, to the south of Heritage Farm, was a magnificent stand of white pine. Kent and I were reminded of the Rocky Mountains each time we walked across the needles blanketing the earth below these magnificent trees, stirring up the scent of the pine forest. We knew the history of those woods, and had already discovered the ruins of Colonel Taylor's cabin. One spring day while in the garden, I heard what reminded me of Dad's John Deere B tractor, starting with a slow, low popping and escalating to a faster poppopping sound. Jerry Johnson, a friend and experienced hunter, told me that the noise came from a ruffed grouse, a natural inhabitant of pine woods. This remarkable sound was caused by the male grouse sitting atop a hollow log, drumming his wings to attract a female.

One day, the owner of the pine woods appeared at the house. Because of a divorce settlement, he was being forced to sell the woods, and he wanted SSE to know. There were other alternatives: One was

The south valley adjoining Heritage Farm

to sell the trees to a logger, and he had already priced that out. The other—his sons' suggestion—was to cut up the acreage into several building sites, and for that, too, he already had the plans. How did this person know us so well? He knew SSE would have to buy the woods.

After moving to the farm in the spring of 1987, our family quickly became familiar with the borders. Before long I learned where to find morel mushrooms, wild plums, blackcap raspberries, and blackberries. And just as my siblings and I did at our parents' place, our children made the farm their playground. The girls discovered springs and spent hours playing on the fallen trunk and branches of what they simply called the "fun tree." One afternoon, Tracy, seven, and Carrie, five, discovered a clear spring bubbling out of a bank below the magnificent limestone bluffs beyond our border fence. It was sur-rounded with spring wildflowers, and they named the spot Spring Beauty.

Kent and I explored the whole neighborhood. About eight miles north of us, on Fox Hollow Road, we found a hillside of heaven. Each spring, we made a pilgrimage. We'd drive over early in the evening, park, and walk to the fence to admire a hillside of blooming marsh marigold, its brilliant yellow flowers peeking between the leaves of eastern skunk cabbage. Early in the spring, skunk cabbage emerges as a mottled purple cone that unfolds into fifteen-inch leaves resembling cabbage. In the evening quiet, we could hear water softly dropping from a spring that fed the whole ravine. Anyone who owns such a property should forget about ever possessing it—just leave it and the flowers alone.

In the valley behind the barn at Heritage Farm, many tiny springs oozed along the side of the north slope. Skunk cabbage already grew in these areas, but no marsh marigolds. I knew the conditions were suitable, so one evening I ventured to the site along Fox Hollow Road with a large pail and shovel to fetch just one marsh marigold to transplant below the barn. I didn't real-ize how entrenched the roots would be in the swampy ground. They reached deep and were saturated with water. Somehow I successfully unearthed a specimen and dragged a very heavy bucket to the trunk of my car. I drove down the valley and transplanted the marigold almost directly in one of the small springs, hoping the plant would not notice. (The marigold survived, and it grows in that spot today.) It was nearly dark when I finished, and a blue heron glided beside me. As he let out his evening call, I was as content to end my day as he was to end his.

On my spring walks down the south valley behind the barn, I would usually stop at the fence that bordered SSE's property.

Marigolds from the
2010 Summer Edition

The valley beyond the fence was so spacious you could not tell where it started or ended. One day I noticed a yellow glow coming from the north side of the valley floor. I crossed the fence, walked closer through a swampy area, and realized it was the largest patch of marsh marigolds I had ever seen.

Oddly, we were familiar with this property. In 1986, while on the search for Heritage Farm, we had considered buying the valley from Lloyd and LaVisa Klotz. Kent and I drove the entire property—more than 600 acres—but we entered from the east, its back side. That day, I realized the back side of that property was just over the fence in the backyard of Heritage Farm. When we'd looked at it in 1986, the Klotz property seemed like more land than SSE needed, and there were no functional buildings. A year later, the land was sold to Avitus McCabe, who continued to add more farmland to the perimeter. The property became known as Twin Valleys Farm. Avitus and his wife, Lorraine, lived in Harmony, Minnesota. I met them while gathering signatures for the road-naming project, and asked if they minded our family hiking on the property. They were happy to know we enjoyed the farm.

The valley became an enormous area to explore. Kent and I continued our hikes and found treasure after treasure: hillsides of snow trilliums, bluebells along the clear stream bed, hanging bogs and vistas overlooking the whole valley. The highest spot we designated Inspiration Point. We followed grassed-over roads that once led through the valley, connecting over twenty different farms. We found remnants of old homesteads: rusty handles from water pumps, piles of rotten boards, stone foundations and the remains of a pioneer orchard on a homestead. Inside the safe arms of the Twin Valleys, it felt like another world. Even standing at the edge, you could feel the quietness seep into you.

Bill McLain, whose family was among the original settlers in the neighborhood, told us that his great-grandfather had been a neighbor

Ancient White Park cattle grazing in the pastures on Twin Valleys Farm

to Colonel Taylor in the late 1800s and had worked for the colonel. Bill's Great-Aunt Nettie remembered playing and going "nutting" with the Taylor daughters in the fall. Back then, the north and south valleys were beginning to be split into ten-acre woodlots and thirty- to eighty-acre farm parcels. Bill thought that at one point there were more than thirty families living in the two valleys. On a drive one day, Bill's father, Fred, pointed out a spot about 200 yards from Canoe Creek where a wooden stage once stood. They called it the Bowery. "In the summer, all the families from both valleys would meet to dance and listen to fiddle music," he said. "The parents along with their children walked down, bringing picnics and homemade wine and other drinks. It was always a point of pride to see who could make the best moonshine. Lanterns were hung around the dance area and up and down the valleys to guide them home. But no one ever made it back to their farms before sunrise."

As people started moving west, the woodlots were cleared and neighbors bought adjacent properties. In 1874, Colonel Taylor had close to 720 acres. Philip Halse purchased a portion of Colonel Taylor's Pine Spring Farm. In the 1905 map of Canoe Township, that portion of the property appeared as "Evergreen Farms." Eventually there were only three farms remaining. The two valleys were put back together by Lloyd Klotz, and then purchased by Avitus and Lorraine McCabe. The McCabes never allowed anyone to purchase any part of the property; they wanted to keep the land in one piece. But when Avitus passed away in 1992, his family did not want the responsibility of such a large property.

So once again, what adjoined us could be broken into parcels, never to be put back together. We could think of many reasons the property was important to SSE. To garden organically, it was essential to be surrounded with a natural habitat for birds, beneficial insects, and pollinators, to have a buffer for our gardens against spray drift, space to rotate gardens, more pasture land, and plenty of greens for the deer and rabbits to eat.

If SSE could secure this land, we'd add 716 acres contiguous to the 173-acre Heritage Farm and ensure that 889 acres of land would be safe for preservation projects in a nonprofit setting. But was purchasing the Twin Valleys financially possible? And was it necessary to fulfill the mission of Seed Savers Exchange? Kent and I felt we needed concrete reasons if we were to convince anyone that SSE should purchase more land. Early in the life and growth of SSE, when it was just Kent and me, we acted on instinct. Now SSE had a staff and facilities in place. We certainly did not want to jeopardize the security of Heritage Farm and the livelihoods of the many families who worked there.

I have a file in my office labeled "Inspiration," and one quotation it contains is by Aristotle: "Educating the mind without educating

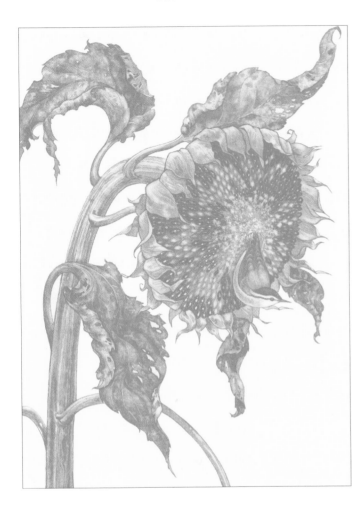

Sunflower
and nuthatch

the heart is not education at all." Heritage Farm was already educating the mind by providing living classrooms in the orchard and gardens, demonstrating diversity and seed preservation. But Kent and I felt strongly that SSE had to secure these valleys, free of noise, power lines, roads, and human presence for as far as you could see. Its silence was broken only by the occasional screeching overhead of a red-tailed hawk, or, if you listened attentively, perhaps the laughter from families working in the gardens or walking down to the Bowery for a summer evening dance. This was education for the heart.

The tract was among the last of its kind in Iowa; in one hundred years, a large piece of rural land protected by a nonprofit organization would be a precious jewel. But what foundation has ever included "education of the heart" in their grant guidelines? Maryanne Mott and Herman Warsh have had faith in our judgment since the early 1970s and helped SSE achieve great things when no one else was noticing. Kent and I had driven them around the property many times when they came to Iowa to visit, pointing out its history and beauty. We filled them in on our hopes. After some consideration, they agreed that the land should not be broken up and would provide valuable options in the future. It was decided that Herman and Maryanne would arrange to purchase the property and hold onto it until Seed Savers could take it over.

The Avitus McCabe Estate land auction was held on Monday, July 6, 1992, at noon at Nob Hill Supper Club, just up the road from Heritage Farm. Avitus had also purchased farms and other properties across the road from the Twin Valleys, and the auction involved a total of 1,500 acres. The 716-acre Twin Valleys property had been broken into twenty-three units. Under terms of the auction, bidders could bid on any parcel separately. Then the property as a whole was to be offered, but the bid for it had to be greater than the total of the bids for the twenty-three individual parcels. The process was called a MultParSell auction.

Wes Henthorne, the ranch manager for Maryanne and Herman, came to Iowa for the auction. In a recent conversation, I asked Wes if he remembered that visit. "I sure do," he said. "I remember being upgraded at the car rental place and I drove down to Decorah from Minneapolis in a black Buick Road Master. I must have been a bit pre-occupied with the upcoming auction, because I checked the speedometer at one point and it sure didn't feel like it, but I was driving nearly 100 miles per hour. So I slowed down."

"I had a letter with a line of credit from the bank in Montana," he went on. "Actually, I had several letters for different amounts, and was prepared to use the appropriate amount needed to purchase the whole property." I asked if he was nervous, and he said, "No, not really. I come from a long line of auctioneers. My great-grandfather was in the business and the first sale bill in our family archives is from 1706."

On the day of the auction, the supper club parking lot was full of cars and pickups. Kent, Wes, and I found a place to sit at one of the long tables and listened to the auctioneer's instructions. Then the bidding started. When it came to bid on the whole Twin Valleys property, Wes started off by putting in a strong bid to let people know he was serious.

Kent and I hadn't told anyone about Wes coming into town; we felt we would be in a better position if no one was prepared to bid on the whole property but us. As it turned out, no one was expecting bids on the whole property. Wes caught everyone off guard. People gathered to pool their money together to get the individual parcels higher in price. But every time it came back to bidding on the whole, Wes could always bid more. Soon it was obvious that he meant business and the others stopped bidding.

I have never felt that our dreams for the property were more worthy than the plans of the people who bid on smaller pieces, but there was an overriding feeling of responsibility to keep this land in one piece. Today Seed Savers Exchange is the privileged caretaker of the silence, two valleys, and many patches of skunk cabbage and marsh marigolds.

Maryanne Mott and Herman Warsh

In the early 1980s, when SSE was focused on a mission of saving seeds, the CS Fund in Freestone, California, had started a mission of its own. In 1981, Herman Warsh and his wife, Maryanne Mott, formed a private foundation dedicated to defending democracy, preventing the commoditization of life, and protecting environmental health. The CS Fund was one of the early leaders in the foundation world to recognize the importance of preserving biodiversity, especially the genetic diversity contained in agricultural seeds. The CS Fund understood the value of SSE's work, possibly even before we did.

SSE's story is about dreams and about individuals who believed in those dreams—family, friends, and those who provided financial support. Herman and Maryanne were two of the earliest and most influential. From those early days in Missouri to Heritage Farm in Iowa, the CS Fund has been a constant source of support.

Herman and Maryanne even opened their home to many non-profit organizations for use as a meeting site or retreat. Their home was the 9,000-acre B Bar Ranch near Emigrant, Montana, set among the 10,000-foot peaks of the Gallatin range in the Tom Miner Basin and adjoining the northern boundary of Yellowstone National Park. It is a place of spectacular beauty, and the CS Fund is committed to protecting this extraordinary landscape. In August 2000, SSE's board held a long-range planning retreat at the B Bar, and our family vacationed at the ranch several times. We all rode horses up mountain passes, spotted moose in the willow swamps, and were impressed by the clawing marks high on a tree, made by a Yellowstone grizzly. (Grizzlies can reach up to ten feet while standing on their back legs.)

When Herman died in the spring of 2006, the world lost a gentle spirit and a real crusader for justice for all. In June 2009, I returned to the ranch to see Maryanne for the first time since Herman's death. My daughter Carrie and her husband, Ryan, on their way to Iowa from San Diego, joined us there. Herman's walking sticks were still leaning in a corner of the entryway to the house. But my sadness was quickly replaced with memories of cheerful morning hikes up into the basin with Herman, whistling while walking the dogs and listening to elk bugle. We had a delightful visit with Maryanne along with her two new yellow Labrador pups, Barley and Buddha.

On our first morning at the ranch, I walked into the kitchen to find Maryanne baking a coffee cake in her beloved Aga range, a red-enameled masterpiece. Carrie, Ryan, Maryanne, and the pups had been up since 6 a.m. They had hiked to a mountain pasture to drive the saddle horses down to the corrals by the barn for the day. The spring grass was lush at the higher elevation and the horses would overeat if left for the entire day.

After breakfast we all took a long walk down to the Reed Place, one of the original homesteads settled in the basin of the B Bar in 1906. A small herd of Suffolk Punch draft horses grazed in the meadow beside the stream, and in the corral next to the Reed Barn several mares stood with new foals by their side. The ranch raises and works Suffolk Punch draft horses to preserve and improve the breed and increase their numbers. Maryanne and I reminisced about the winter Kent and I went cross-country skiing. The Suffolk groomed the trails and then pulled us all in a bobsled to the top of the mountains. We skied all day. If that had been in Iowa we would never have lasted. But under the big blue sky, close to the sun, with the snow and air so dry, it was effortless.

The meals at the ranch have always been memorable. In 1990, when our family was invited to visit, the ranch gardens consisted of a few double-dug raised beds, and the staff was beginning to experiment with heirloom vegetables that could be successfully grown for cooking at the guest ranch. In 2009, I passed by a much larger garden of raised beds, encased with a very tall deer fence; three young women were weeding the potato patch. The crew proudly reported that the gardens and greenhouse at the B Bar were about to be certified organic.

Curious how the heirloom varieties were producing (invaluable information for other high-altitude gardeners growing SSE's varieties), I asked the lead horticulturist about her main challenges. She didn't have to think long: "Gardening in a climate that could potentially have freezing temperatures every month is tricky. On the plus side, there are not a lot of bugs that survive, either."

Lunch brought evidence of her success. The ranch chef had prepared a cold duck salad served on a bed of mixed greens, all grown in the B Bar greenhouse. Sweet yellow cherry tomatoes called Blondköpfchen, or "Little Blond Girl," were sprinkled atop the salad, which contained many SSE varieties that I recognized: Gold Rush and Red Mascara lettuce, chopped Lacinato kale, Sylvetta arugula, and beet greens, which turned out to be from McGregor's Favorite. This beet, first grown in 1892, is offered in the SSE catalog, but I had never tasted it. The previous night's dinner had featured roasted root vegetables, including these beets, which were roasted unpeeled—the sweet skin melted in your mouth.

The horticulturist said the Blondköpfchen tomatoes were grown in the greenhouse at this time of the year. "We would never be without them," she said. "The tiny tomatoes are clustered together like statice flowers, never crack, and produce large quantities." I felt a sense of parental pride when I saw SSE varieties performing so well in this high altitude.

Maryanne told me that the CS Fund's original interest was in saving the genetic diversity found in minor breeds of livestock; she and Herman had worked closely with the American Minor Breeds Conservancy (AMBC). "We began examining what we saw as being threatened in the world," she said, and decided that many organizations were already working to preserve natural systems. "This probing became an intellectual process that led us to seeds. On further examination, we found there was more benefit and risk involved in seeds, more hierarchy in seeds."

So she and Herman expanded their foundation's mission to include genetic preservation of seeds. The CS Fund has a major grants

Chioggia beet

program titled Food Sovereignty: "Our focus is on soil, seeds, and pollinators, and we are especially mindful of the inextricable bond between culture and agriculture."

Maryanne said she wasn't certain how they first learned of Kent and me, but did recall that in the early 1980s, Marty Teitel, then the fund's executive director, brought photos of our Missouri garden and Aaron helping out as a youngster. "We found that very interesting and decided to send Kristin McKendall, our program officer, to Missouri to check it out."

I told her how nervous we'd felt about a visitor from a foundation in California coming to our house in Missouri. It was a first for us, and we didn't know what to expect. Certainly we wanted to make a good impression. Kristin's report must have been positive, because in 1983 SSE was invited to submit a proposal for funding. That initial application was to hire our first employee in Missouri to help finish the *Garden Seed Inventory* and buy seed stock of 760 endangered commercial varieties and the equipment (freezer, heat sealer, and sealable pouches for frozen storage) to store seeds properly. This was the beginning of a long friendship and partnership with the CS Fund.

I asked Maryanne if there were concerns about SSE's lack of a track record. "No," she replied. "Herman and I had no worries about the lack of a track record, we were glad to be able to help you build one. Kent presented well-thought-out proposals that were powerful and compelling. You and Kent kept the vision and kept delivering."

She added: "We believed it could work. We felt your organization was strong, yet not dependent on a single leader—we bet on solid people involved with the whole effort, not the shining star." Maryanne also mentioned that SSE never missed a granting report deadline, which foundations always appreciated. I was astonished that grantees would not report on time. "That seems unthinkable!" I exclaimed. "One would think so," she responded, "but you would be amazed how often reports are late."

The CS Fund has lent SSE money for five land acquisitions, beginning in 1987 with Heritage Farm and ending with the land for the office site in 1993. I told Maryanne that she must have had doubts about our request to acquire the Twin Valleys, a purchase of more than 700 acres that must have looked as if we were overextending our ambitions. Without hesitation, she answered: "Not really. The properties always seemed to make real sense for your growth and needs at the time."

She acknowledged that she and Herman had to ponder the Twin Valleys purchase. "I don't think we doubted the role the land could eventually play in your overall program, but we weren't sure you would be able to bring all the other people and funds on board to make it happen, as you were just coming off a major capital campaign and this was going to be a whole new load to carry. This did not mean we had doubts about you guys but simply that we knew you were going to be taking on a big challenge . . . again! But it was clear that if we ended up holding the land and needing to sell it off, it had great inherent value. So even as a straight investment, it was a sound step to take. Herman and I never intended to be involved in the management; SSE had to eventually take over the property." It was good that Maryanne and Herman were patient, because SSE took nearly a decade, until 2002, to complete the acquisition.

SSE has also partnered with the B Bar Ranch to preserve and improve the Ancient White Park cattle breed. "The B Bar Ranch has 9,000 deeded acres and 11,000 acres of national forest we can use for grazing," Maryanne said. "It just seemed logical that we should be using this land to preserve a rare breed or two. At the same time, we needed our land usage program to be demonstrating appropriate rotational livestock grazing and we could utilize the cattle as a tool to enhance the health of the range.

"I think Herman gradually got Wes Henthorne, the cattle manager for the ranch, past his reservations about a strange breed of cattle.

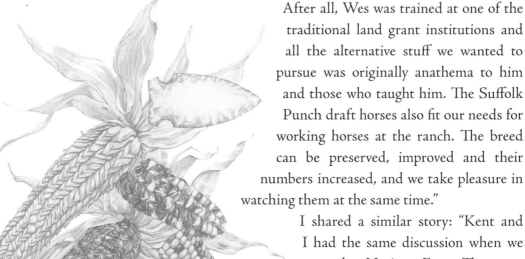

Kokopelli and
Indian corn

After all, Wes was trained at one of the traditional land grant institutions and all the alternative stuff we wanted to pursue was originally anathema to him and those who taught him. The Suffolk Punch draft horses also fit our needs for working horses at the ranch. The breed can be preserved, improved and their numbers increased, and we take pleasure in watching them at the same time."

I shared a similar story: "Kent and I had the same discussion when we moved to Heritage Farm. There was about thirty acres of fenced pastures, a perfect setup for a small herd of cattle." Kent had been interested in Ancient White Park cattle because they were rare and had such a rich history. The breed originated some two thousand years ago on what are now the British Isles. The cattle were shipped to North America at the start of World War II for fear of a Nazi invasion. The herd resided at the Toronto Zoo, the Bronx Zoo, and the King Ranch in Texas before being purchased by John and Marilyn Moeckly, who lived near Des Moines.

One hot day in July 1987, our family went down to visit the Moecklys. Ancient White Park cattle are somewhat primitive-looking, with lyre-shaped horns on both bulls and cows. The animals are white, with black ears and some color on their feet and noses and around the eyes. The adorable calves reminded the kids of pandas. SSE started buying heifer calves that year. In 1989, the Moecklys decided to focus on Black Angus, and wanted to sell all of their Ancient White Park cattle. Seed

Savers Exchange was not set up for the herd, but we told Marilyn we knew about a ranch in Montana. Maryanne and Herman sent Wes, their cattle manager, to Iowa to purchase the remainder of the herd.

As Herman and Maryanne became more involved with SSE's work and our family, we became friends as well as partners. "Herman and I felt organizations that grew with the attention of a whole family had a soul, a culture, an organization with a personality," Maryanne said.

A nice rhubarb patch growing in the ranch's garden reminded me of Maryanne's first visit to Iowa. It was the spring of 1989. Jessica was just a year old and I felt overwhelmed with the activities of four other children. Late one afternoon, Kent and Maryanne returned from photographing the Ancient White Park cattle. We sat on the lawn looking at the barn below, and I passed out some ice cream sandwiches left over from Tracy's second-grade field trip that afternoon. Maryanne said, "Oh, a little treat before dinner?" and I replied, "No, actually this *is* dinner." We all laughed. We had a proper dinner later that evening, and a rhubarb crisp for dessert—Maryanne's first taste of this spring tonic. I told her of rhubarb's hardiness, and said it would surely survive in her mountain garden. I don't know if it was the idea of ice cream sandwiches for dinner or her introduction to rhubarb that broke the ice, but we bonded over rhubarb crisp and our families have been friends ever since.

Today the generous contribution and spirit of Maryanne and Herman live on at Seed Savers Heritage Farm and beyond through a program called "Herman's Garden." Although SSE has long had a donation program that provided free seed to organizations and community gardens, the program had no name. I remembered Herman commenting on his days as a teacher. "I was the one to whom they sent all the 'difficult' kids," he said. "I loved them. What others saw as problems, I saw as needs and opportunities."

Before he died, he requested that there be no fuss or flowers; he simply asked that his friends do a good deed in his name. What better name for SSE's seed donation program? In 2010, Herman's Garden distributed more than 36,000 seed packets to around 400 gardens throughout the country.

Growing Strong

Over the years SSE has been honored to work with many talented and generous board members. Our current board—in addition to Amy Goldman, Cary Fowler, Rosalind Creasy, and David Cavagnaro—includes Vice-Chair Neil Hamilton, who is Distinguished Professor of Law and Director of the Agricultural Law Center at Drake University Law School. Neil has taught law for thirty years and is the author of numerous books and articles. A board member since 1997, he has wisely guided SSE through a great deal of growth.

Rob Johnston, Jr., founder of Johnny's Selected Seeds, enriches SSE with the knowledge he has gained in his more than thirty-five years as a plant breeder and influential advocate of organic gardening. Keith Crotz, an agricultural literature historian, who attended his first SSE campout in 1986, has enlarged the organization's intellectual storehouse by facilitating the donation and further collection development of the Robert Becker Memorial Library. In 2010, three new members joined the board: George DeVault, Glenn Drowns, and Larry Grimstad. Deborah Madison, with more than a dozen books on cooking with seasonal fruits and vegetables to her name, recently stepped off the board to become an advisor for SSE.

The organization's dreams have certainly challenged its board. There was the color seed catalog and the retail outreach stores, but the biggest and riskiest venture had to be the purchase of Twin Valleys Farm. Neil, along with the rest of the board, was very cautious about

taking on the financial responsibility of buying and maintaining 716 acres of land. All of the board members were touched by the beauty of the property and believed the future of SSE would be enhanced by its addition. But board members have to be prudent, too, and they were concerned about the financial health of SSE. They needed assurances that raising $1.9 million would not detract from the organization's primary mission.

In 2003, Neil was serving on the boards of two conservation groups, Seed Savers Exchange and the Iowa Natural Heritage Foundation (INHF). He was able to coordinate a program between SSE, INHF, and the USDA's Natural Resource Conservation Service that resulted in substantial financial support for the Twin Valleys Farm capital campaign. These three organizations worked together to put

Rosalind Creasy photographing the Outhouse hollyhocks in the display garden at Heritage Farm the 716 acres of the Twin Valleys into the Federal Farmland Protection Program, which is aimed at promoting both agricultural diversity and wild species.

The Federal Farmland Protection Program works with willing landowners and pays approximately 50 percent of the value of all development rights on a piece of land. The payment under the farmland protection program supplemented SSE's newly launched campaign to raise funds for the purchase of Twin Valleys Farm. In addition to requiring that development rights be extinguished, the federal rules require recipients to develop a long-term conservation plan for the property. Both of these requirements were in line with the goals of Seed Savers Exchange, so it was a victory for all sides.

SSE's conservation plan incorporates both agricultural practices and protection of the site's natural features. Plan elements include creating isolation gardens for renewing heirloom seeds; developing eco-friendly rotational grazing for the Ancient White Park cattle; reconstructing native plant communities, including prairies and savannas; restoring streams; planting riparian buffers along two coldwater streams; preserving the rare geological formations that derive from the Ice Age; and restoring existing buildings to use for agriculture, education, and visitor services.

"In many ways, what Seed Savers is doing is the epitome of farmland protection. They are making sure we have the genetic diversity in our food system," says Lisa Hein, program and planning director at the Iowa Natural Heritage Foundation. "By protecting the entire Twin Valleys with a conservation easement, those diversity goals include the natural systems on the land."

The real victor was Twin Valleys: the land was purchased to prevent development. The Iowa Natural Heritage Foundation monitors SSE annually, making sure that no part of Twin Valleys is ever sold or developed. This property will be protected after Kent's involvement and mine, and through future guardians of SSE. We intended to raise half of the funds for Twin Valleys as an organization before we involved our members. With Neil's efforts and Amy Goldman's generous donation to kick off the campaign, we leaped past the starting line.

That campaign began in 2003, and was finished four years later, in 2007. Many partners helped Seed Savers reach that goal. We crossed the finish line with support from SSE members, the Lillian Goldman Charitable Trust, the Wallace Genetic Foundation, the Diggers' Club, the 1772 Foundation, and the Ceres Trust.

The Unexpected Happens

"You two will end up getting divorced," a longtime friend told me at a conference in 1994. I was dumbfounded. But hers was a voice of experience. She was co-founder of a Midwestern nonprofit organization with many similarities to Seed Savers Exchange. And she was recently divorced, after raising her family, nurturing a nonprofit organization, and living in the middle of projects and staff.

On the drive back from the conference, I told Kent about her prediction. He replied, "It'll never happen to us," and I agreed. Not in a million years. We were not that couple. We'd already survived homesteading with cistern water, building a house from the ground up, raising five children, founding a nonprofit organization, and doing it all on a shoestring budget. A decade later, in 2004, I was pleased with what we had accomplished but not surprised, considering the amount of energy we had poured into the Seed Savers Exchange. But to my immense surprise, if not my friend's, my marriage did not survive the process. Kent and I were divorced in 2004, after thirty-three years of marriage.

There were warning signs. Our children clearly understood that our life was out of balance. On most vacations, they told us we were

The barn at Heritage Farm, Decorah, Iowa

not allowed to talk about work, though the ban was usually honored only for the first day. When we did manage a vacation—not an annual event—it was usually centered on a business commitment, so ignoring work was hard. For years we juggled two all-consuming causes: a family and a nonprofit organization. There was precious little time for Kent and me to recharge our marriage. It's tough to stay married in normal circumstances, whatever those are. For us, the extra stress of mixing business and family was, ultimately, a strain the marriage could not bear.

Our vision had become a serious commitment: Kent and I had long since given up outside jobs, committing ourselves to the financial health of SSE. For years, Seed Savers pinched every penny—twice! There seemed always to be a cash-flow crisis. Initially I worked for no salary, and Kent's was minimal. There were no benefits like health insurance, sick leave, vacation time, or a retirement plan. SSE had a line of credit at the bank that was used regularly, especially at year's end. Often we lost sleep wondering if we would make the next payroll or find money for snow tires. We delayed paying bills for as long as possible: a constant juggling act. The catalog would be printed in October and we would not finish paying the printer until May.

We rarely succeeded in finding time that did not involve work or children. There were always school concerts, Nordic dances, wrestling matches, track meets, or games of volleyball, baseball, softball, or football. In between, there were lots of practices and rides to town.

It was also impossible to physically escape work; we literally lived in the middle of it on Heritage Farm. The SSE office was above us on the north, the orchard on the south, and gardens, staff, and visitors all around. I had beans in my living room, Martha Stewart in my kitchen, and strangers shampooing in my shower. Employees worked in our home for nearly twenty years. We held board meetings, entertained potential grant-givers, visitors, and SSE campout attendees there. We operated a mini B & B—only mine was bed and a banana in the morning. Seed Savers Exchange was our sixth child.

This other dependent grew and changed over time, and as it grew, the required day-to-day attention grew as well. People made telling observations: in the early 1980s, John Hartman commented that SSE had "a tiger by the tail"; John Swenson described it as "an organism with a life of its own."

In 1990, after Kent received the MacArthur Fellowship, he began to travel nationally and internationally. Our roles at the time seemed to be balanced. He was the front person, comfortable with travel, speaking, and being the public figure for SSE. I held down the home front. With a business and five children, it was not possible for both of us to travel. And we were both exhausted—me from being the "married single mother" and him from traveling. There was tension, but we started to accept stress as a normal part of our life. That should have been a huge red flag.

I recognize we could have, probably should have, done things differently. I did expect the ending of the story to be, "And they lived happily ever after." Though we didn't know where we were heading, the path was beautiful and exciting. It would have been difficult to know what to change, and even if we had wanted to, maybe the change wasn't ours to make.

The path remains beautiful today, with one big difference. My grown children are close to me; they're my best friends. But I am now traveling with a family of 13,000-plus, instead of the one I started out with. We know where and how the road began, and we know that there is more beauty to look forward to. And happy endings are still possible.

Evolution

On May 5, 2004, I received a call from my lawyer; the divorce papers were ready to sign. I wanted to get this final act behind me, so even though it was Saturday I drove into town, feeling a bit as if I were going to attend a funeral. It was 10 a.m. and the church bells were tolling, adding to the funereal atmosphere.

On my way to the lawyer's office, I walked past a group of cheerful young women smoking outside of a hair salon. The bride-to-be was wearing blue jeans and a shirt, her tiara perfectly intertwined in her just-styled hair, the veil framing her face. She looked so happy. Seeing the veil, I wistfully remembered my wedding day, when Grandpa Ott put my white veil on Grandma and we danced in their living room.

I signed the papers and headed back to the farm, feeling terribly alone. But I still had my family—the youngest, Jessica, was a sixteen-year-old with a new driver's license. And I had Maggie, a beautiful yellow Labrador from a breeder in Blue Earth, Minnesota, who had bred the dogs I enjoyed so much at Maryanne Mott's B Bar Ranch. She was my "divorce puppy," acquired to fill in some of the void.

The first clue that this may have been a mistake was finding the book Maryanne had sent me, *The Art of Disciplining a Puppy*, chewed up on the living room floor. The chewing escalated to the license plate on my car and then to tree trunks in the front yard. Maggie was a handful by day, but we enjoyed glorious walks in the evening in the Twin Valleys.

The spring of 2004 arrived as usual. Bluebirds returned to their house in the hollyhock patch, the soil warmed, the spring rains came and brought my garden back to life. We were serenaded by peepers, and fat asparagus shoots started poking through the ground. Grandpa Ott's morning glories came up abundantly, and began their climb up the side of the barn. In the display garden, Grandma Einck's dill and borage reappeared, the perennials poked their foliage up through the earth, and the self-seeding annuals sprouted. The last to come up, predictably, were the Kiss-Me-Over-the-Garden-Gate and the verbenas. I love the display garden. This space, originally a graveled cow lot beside the barn, had over the twenty years I worked on it been transformed into what seemed to me a mini-paradise.

Spring peeper and asparagus

The preservation gardens were planted, the orchard was in bloom. White lilacs looked gorgeous in the front yard, and the visitor center was stocked with beautiful seeds, plants, books, and merchandise. Visitors started arriving, and Seed Savers Exchange was ready for the new season. So normal, and yet to me everything seemed different.

In February, Kent had informed the SSE board of our impending divorce. I know the news was a shock to the board. Kent and I were masters at never letting our personal

problems show. With the best of intentions, we assured the board that we would be able to function as we had in the past. We both knew we owed that much to the board, and to all of SSE's members, the people who trusted us, and our family. Everyone had worked too hard over the years for us to drop the ball now.

Even so, my new role was the biggest challenge yet in all my years of working with SSE. Kent was executive director, I was associate director, and we definitely struggled with communication. While he had moved out of the farmhouse, we both worked at the office as we had for so many years. Each day that I walked up the hill through the bur oak savanna from the farmhouse to the office felt surreal. Over the years that followed, I got either used to the situation or numb to it. SSE's projects kept moving forward, but Kent and I had less and less contact with each other and I began to feel isolated. The board may have felt the same, and tension definitely grew.

In many ways my voice had always been half of Kent's; we complemented each other. Now I needed to find my own voice. I was surviving, but feeling increasingly alienated from the organization—more like an employee than a founder. Then one day in 2006 I read an article on the Internet called "Founder's Syndrome: An Affliction for Which There Is Rarely Immunity," by Henry D. Lewis, a professional fund-raiser. And I started to understand.

The syndrome, Lewis wrote, typically plagues mom-and-pop operations: entrepreneurial, seat-of-the-pants organizations very much like SSE. Their founders are dynamic and often forced to make crisis-driven decisions with little input from others. Such founders motivate people. They bring the organization through the tough times of start-up. They juggle growth spurts and financial crises, all the while soothing various egos and keeping the focus. They have the vision. They know their members' needs and are passionate about meeting them. Such founders are strong assets for getting a fledgling nonprofit off the ground.

I could see where this was heading. The difficulty, Lewis said, was that the founders developed a feeling of ownership of the organization. And it's true that SSE was deeply personal. Kent and I devoted our lives to creating the organization, went without money, sleep, and privacy. We gave it our sweat and our tears. We even borrowed against the family car. We envisioned the organization, and worked solo for so many years that SSE did feel like our own.

But the organization was not ours. It was its own entity. And there was another message that was difficult to acknowledge: The world owes me nothing for founding this organization. It's not about me. In the long run, what we poured into the organization did not matter. Ouch, that hurt a bit. But it was true. It was never, or should never have been, about our egos or emotional needs. It was not about what we sacrificed to make it all work. It was about the mission that led us to create SSE in the first place: To save seeds.

I looked again at SSE's mission statement: "Seed Savers Exchange is saving the world's diverse, but endangered garden heritage for future generations by building a network of people committed to collecting, conserving, and sharing heirloom seeds and plants, while educating people about the value of genetic and cultural diversity."

Of course Kent and I trusted that SSE as a nonprofit would live beyond our involvement. We had created an amazing gift for the world. But now that we had given this gift, it was no longer ours. It belonged to others, not us. I understood that. But knowing how I *should* feel and how I really *did* feel did not quite match up. These were tough messages to receive, let alone accept. Kent and I had experienced many of SSE's growing pains through the years, but we could always discuss the changes and support each other through unpleasant situations. Now we were facing a painful stage in Seed Savers' development, but we were not facing it together.

And of course there was the more mundane stress of simply being a divorced couple living near each other and trying to work together.

Whatever the factors, SSE's management began to deteriorate on many levels. The board continued to be supportive, at one point suggesting we attend mediation sessions in an effort to get back on track. Kent and I had encouraged these people to become board members because of their professional qualifications. The truth was that we really needed their level-headedness, more now than at any time in our previous history.

I began to withdraw more from the daily operations as I realized I really had no control over the workings at SSE or the relationship that Kent had with the board, staff, and SSE members. But to ease the situation for all, in July 2006 we both resigned from the board. I remained as associate director, tending the display garden, managing the Lillian Goldman Visitors Center, developing events and the calendar, writing articles and copy for the catalog and website—focusing on the areas that needed my attention.

This strange chapter of SSE, which began with the announcement of our impending divorce in February 2004, continued to become more painful. I began to feel like a parent in a dysfunctional family, and I sensed that there were problems between the board and Kent. At the end of October 2007 I was out of the country visiting a friend when I learned that the board had unanimously decided to terminate Kent's employment. I was shocked and saddened. I knew this decision had not been made quickly or without giving Kent every chance to resolve the issues. These people on the board, in addition to the many talents they offered the organization, were our friends.

I also knew this would come as a surprise to others—especially those who were not aware of all the changes at SSE over the previous four years. Some members said it made no sense and seemed unfair. Some feared it could destroy the organization. Personnel matters are confidential, of course, so I was not privy to the details and could not fully address the first two of those concerns. But I could offer one assurance: SSE was stronger than its founders. It was a world-class organization, and it would survive.

When I returned to work the next week and walked up the hill to the office, my role had again changed back to a maternal one: with the board's counsel, I endeavored to be a steadying force during the greatest change in the organization's history.

In November 2007, the board voted to begin the search for a new executive director. I expected that, of course, but was taken aback to learn the new executive director would live in the farmhouse. Of course, that made sense. It was not really the Whealy family home; it belonged to SSE. George DeVault, the new executive director, who was hired in October 2008, should live there, just

as the previous one had. But the process of moving the paraphernalia of twenty-one years, five children, and a life dedicated to building SSE was wrenching.

Cleaning out closets and an attic was also therapeutic. My past has been filled with more richness than I ever could have imagined. More important, there is a future. People and Seed Savers Exchange

The display garden next to the barn at Heritage Farm in the early morning light

are both resilient. Kent's and my greatest accomplishment, aside from raising five wonderful children, was converting a dream into reality and inspiring others to keep that dream real. I am proud that our vision started the organization thirty-six years ago. But we have evolved over the years, and matured. Perhaps it is we who have changed, and all that remains unchanged is the vision. And that is as it should be.

A Rooster Step

In wildness is the preservation of the world.
HENRY DAVID THOREAU

This story began with a child in northeast Iowa listening to the sayings of her German grandparents. I remember Grandma Einck's observation that each day gets a rooster step longer after winter begins. The stride of a rooster, especially our bantams, isn't much to speak of—more like a baby step. But by the end of January, it might stay light till 5:15 p.m. And of course, by the first day of summer, the days seem longer by a thousand rooster steps.

Grandma Einck's wisdom has come to mind many times in my adult life. Last spring, while working in the visitors' center, I overheard a conversation between two women. "I wonder where they get all the seed," one of them said. "How did they start Seed Savers Exchange?" Behind the counter, I thought about how "we"—meaning Kent and I—had become "they." It was like having a child grow up and become an independent person with a new identity. How did that happen so suddenly? Well, it didn't happen suddenly. It happened with the incremental certainty of a rooster's step.

In 2011, I drive to work and begin my day in a parking lot filled with unfamiliar vehicles. Trying to remember all the new names, I greet people walking to and from the buildings and gardens (these days the office area and the visitors' center area are sometimes referred to as the upper and lower campus). Most of the people joining us today are new employees or members. Some were not even born when SSE began thirty-six years ago. Change is, of course, part of growing up. But it seems important to pass along the story of how SSE was conceived as well as why.

Grandpa Ott's morning glory vining its way around a lawn chair beside the barn at Heritage Farm

Kent and I operated on instinct, but we were sincere and we had a purpose. Somehow we found an effortless way to communicate. We opened our home in Missouri, and later in Iowa, to many people who were treated as family and indeed became family over the years as we shared humor, friendship, and food. To us, seeds were always connected to people—people whose stories, no less than good soil and spring rains, brought those seeds to life.

My life has been filled with new friends, seeds, gardening, food preserving, bearing and rearing children. I have dreaded snowstorms, frozen pipes, and muddy roads, helped build a house, carried firewood, and worked to further what I still regard as one of the world's most important missions. Seed Savers Exchange got where it is today partly through vision, partly through love, partly through hard work, and partly—maybe even mainly—through endurance. Those factors add up to spirit, the spirit that has conceived and nurtured SSE and needs to be felt and maintained today by those who join, save seeds, and visit Heritage Farm.

Just as Pine Spring Farm was home for Colonel Taylor's family more than one hundred years ago, Heritage Farm has become the "home place," not just for an organization but for an ideal. It overflows with gardens planted with seeds from all over the world. It has woods of white pine where fallen trees are left to grow moss and grouse find hollow logs scattered on the forest floor. Ancient White Park cattle graze in the Twin Valleys, historic apple trees bloom, streams run quietly through protected landscapes. It is a place to witness preservation in every aspect of the world—a refuge that inspires hope and reaffirms our faith in nature.

This Seed Savers story began more than one hundred years ago in Bavaria, where morning glories grew on my ancestors' front porches and tomato plants fruited in their gardens. It began without a plan but with heartfelt determination, and it continues to grow and change in northeast Iowa. After fifteen months, George DeVault resigned his position to return to his own home place in Pennsylvania. Our son, Aaron, filled in until John Torgrimson was appointed President and Executive Director in 2010; John had previously served SSE as Editor of Publications. Aaron's sons will, I believe, have better luck with the "no talking about work rule" than our kids did. And that's good news. Children grow up faster than those rooster steps.

Grandpa Ott's morning glory growing strong

Whatever the state of the world, however bitter the winter, each year the spring peepers sing, lilacs bloom, bluebirds nest in the hollyhock patch, and the morning glories sprout. This place embodies resilience and rebirth. Its roots are strong and grow deeper every year.

NOTES

Page 49: "A front-page story in the *Los Angeles Times* . . ." (Randolph)

53: "About 600 members . . ." (Whealy, "Grant," 45)

59: "About a week later, Kent and I . . ." (Anderson)

62: "So far we'd created . . ." (Whealy, "Introduction," 1984, 1)

66: "In Massachusetts, when I got . . ." (Withee, reprinted in "Seed," 35)

68: "This first delivery of boxes . . ." (Whealy, "Bean," 14)

69: "The large basement was available . . ." (Whealy, "Growers," 1984, 253)

70: "We knew we had more than . . ." (Whealy, "Bean," 14)

70: "The cases were ten drawers high . . ." (Whealy, "Growers," 1984, 253)

73: "He wrote later . . ." (Whealy, "Building," 13)

73: "We thought the inventory . . ." (Whealy, "Introduction (Garden Seed)," 7)

81: "Every summer we'd attended . . ." (Whealy, "Fifth")

90: "Our next step was to rent . . ." (Whealy, "Preservation," 122)

90: "The SSE garden was planted . . ." (Whealy, "Preservation," 124)

109: "At the first SSE campout in Decorah . . ." (Woods, reprinted in "Tom," 54)

112: "As more homesteaders arrived, Kelly complained . . ." (Pine)

113: "The land and residence became known as Pine Spring Farm . . ." (Pine)

114: "A chapter titled 'Pleasure Resorts' . . ." (Alexander, 298)

115: "One large area was kept uncultivated . . ." ("Death")

115: "There was also a fine park . . ." ("Unique")

115: "An item in *The Decorah Republican* . . ." ("Can't")

124: "Dan Bussey, SSE's orchard advisor . . ." (Bussey, 50)

125: "SSE's collection is based . . ." (Bussey, 49)

125: "Today many breeders . . ." (Bussey, 51)

125: "To propagate a favored variety . . ." (Bussey, 50)

126: "In February 1989, a small group . . ." (Sliwa, "Historic," 1989, 50, 53)

127: "The orchard was divided into three blocks . . ." (Sliwa, "Historic," 1990, 12)

127: "Dan Zook and his crew . . ." (Sliwa, "Historic," 1990, 12)

128: "Mary K. Northrop and Ole A. Lomen . . ." (Sliwa, "'Apple,'" 41)

128: "Ole O. Lomen maintained his orchard . . ." (Sliwa, "'Apple,'" 42, 46)

129: "Oscar showed David . . ." (Sliwa, "'Apple,'" 42, 46)

132: "Some members of SSE are experienced . . ." (Ashworth, [7])

133: "Do turnips cross with Chinese cabbage . . ." (Ashworth, [7])

133: "She expected to find . . ." (Ashworth, [7])

137: "In 1981, Seed Savers Exchange set up . . ." (Whealy, "Growers," 1982)

138: "By the late 1980s SSE had over 5,000 varieties . . ." (Whealy, "SSE's Network," 113–157)

143: "One of the reasons Kent wanted to travel . . ." (Whealy, "Introduction," 1991)

144: "In those four years . . ." (Woods, "Long-Range," 47)

158: "Kees was known for large grow-outs . . ." (Ogden, 25)

158: "He trialed 13,000 violas . . ." (*Viola*)

158: "There were about 850 varieties . . ." (Ogden, 27)

158: "I was sure he expected me . . ." ("Prickly")

166: "Peaches on the shelf . . ." (Brown, "Canned")

169: "Late that night on the porch . . ." (Goodmann, 11)

169: "I've never played in front . . ." (Whealy, "Third")

172: "On January 3, 1983 . . ." (Cavagnaro, Letter)

175: "Our gorgeous pepper collection . . ." (Luoma)

179: "David had his own take . . ." (Cavagnaro, Fifth, 99)

179: "*The 'amateurs' have been . . .*" (Harlan, Letter)

181: "At the end of the day . . ." (Mooney, 21)

181: "These resources stand between us . . ." (Harlan, "Genetics," 212)

182: "He raised the alarm . . ." (Duffy)

196: "At a meeting in March of 2002 . . ." (Whealy, "Dedication,"14)

197: "The gift would give SSE . . ." (Whealy, "Introduction: Lillian," 7)

214: "I shared a similar story . . ." (Whealy, "History," 92)

SOURCES

Note: Titles of Seed Savers Exchange publications are listed here in their most basic forms: *True Seed Exchange, Seed Savers Exchange, Seed Savers Catalog, Yearbook, Harvest Edition, Spring Edition,* and *Summer Edition.* Actual cover titles vary.

Alexander, W. E. *History of Winneshiek and Allamakee Counties, Iowa.* Sioux City, IA: Western Publishing Co., 1882.

Anderson, Dale. Letter to Kent and Diane Whealy. June 1981.

Ashworth, Suzanne. *Seed to Seed.* Decorah, IA: Seed Saver Publications, 1991.

Brown, Greg. "Canned Goods." *One Night . . .* [CD]. Red House, 1999. Used by permission of the artist.

Bussey, Dan. "Heirloom Apples in Heritage Farm's Orchard." *Harvest Edition,* 1997: 49–60. Used by permission of the author.

"Can't Raise Apples, Eh?" *The Decorah Republican,* August 26, 1870: 1.

Cavagnaro, David. [Fifth Annual Campout] "David Cavagnaro." *Harvest Edition,* 1985: 86–99.

———. Letter to Kent Whealy. January 3, 1983.

"Death of Col. John W. Taylor." *The Decorah Republican,* August 14, 1902: 6.

Dioum, Baba. Address to the Tenth General Assembly of the International Union for Conservation of Nature and Natural Resources. New Delhi, India. November 24–December 1, 1969.

Dorrough, Mrs. Wayne. "Hodgepodge." *True Seed Exchange,* 1978: 228.

Duffy, Andrew. "Biodiversity 'crackpot' wins Pearson Peace Medal—Activist wages war against 'life patents.'" *Ottawa Citizen,* December 16, 1998: A10. Used by permission of Canwest Digital Media/*Ottawa Citizen.*

Fitzgerald, Robert. "Hodgepodge." *True Seed Exchange,* 1978: 228.

Goodmann, Tom. "Saving Seeds; Saving Days." *Summer Edition,* 2003: 9–11. Used by permission of the author.

Harlan, Jack. "Genetics of disaster." *Journal of Environmental Quality* 1972b.1:212–215.

———. Letter to Gary Nabhan. December 23, 1981.

Luoma, John R. "Heirlooms in Your Garden." *Audubon*, 91.6 (November 1989): 46–53.

Mooney, Pat. "The Genesis of the Global Movement." *Harvest Edition*, 1990: 7–21. Used by permission of the author.

Ogden, Shepherd. "Adventures in the Seed Trade." *Harvest Edition*, 2001: 22–35.

"Pine Spring Farm." *The Decorah Republican*, June 23, 1887: 5.

"Prickly Caterpillar." *Seed Savers Catalog*, 2004: 39.

Randolph, Eleanor. "'Bean-Squawk'—Seed Patents: Fears Sprout at Grass Roots." *Los Angeles Times*, June 2, 1980: I-1. Used by permission of the *Los Angeles Times*.

Silva, Becky. Letter to Kent Whealy. June 1, 1988. Used by permission of the author.

Sliwa, David. "'Apple' Lomen's Orchard." *Summer Edition*, 1989: 41–49. Used by permission of the author.

———. "Historic Apple Orchard Becomes a Reality." *Summer Edition*, 1990: 9–16. Used by permission of the author.

———. "Historic Apple Orchard Takes Root at Heritage Farm." *Summer Edition*, 1989: 50–56. Used by permission of the author.

"A Unique Old Landmark Destroyed by Fire." *The Decorah Public Opinion*, April 17, 1907: 1.

"*Viola wittrockiana* Historic Pansies Mixture." *Seed Savers Catalog*, 2001: 52.

Whealy, Kent. "The Bean Men." *Harvest Edition*, 1981: 14.

———. "Building the Heirloom Seed Movement: Campout Speech by Kent Whealy." *Harvest Edition*, 2000: 11–20.

———. "Dedication and Grand Opening of Lillian Goldman Visitors Center." *Summer Edition*, 2005: 10–15.

———. "Fifth Annual Campout Convention." *Harvest Edition*, 1985: 61.

———. Grant Proposal to the Soil and Health Society, 1981. Reprinted in "Grant Proposal." *Seed Savers Exchange*, 1981: 44–49.

———. "The Growers Network." *Yearbook*, 1982: 4.

———. "The Growers Network for 1984." *Yearbook*, 1984: 253.

———. "The History of White Park Cattle in North America." *Harvest Edition*, 1992: 91–105.

———. "Introduction." *Harvest Edition*, 1984: 1–2.

———. "Introduction." *Summer Edition*, 1991: 3.

———. "Introduction: Lillian Goldman Visitors Center." *Summer Edition*, 2004: 7–10.

———. "Introduction (The Garden Seed Inventory)." *Harvest Edition*, 1984: 4–9.

———. "The Preservation Garden." *Harvest Edition*, 1985: 120–133.

———. "SSE's Network of Vegetable Curators." *Harvest Edition*, 1988: 111–157.

———. "Third Benefit Concert by Greg Brown." *Harvest Edition*, 2001: 5.

Withee, John. Presentation to Seed Banks Serving People Workshop, Tucson, Arizona. October 13–14, 1981. Reprinted in "Seed Banks Serving People Workshop," *Harvest Edition*, 1981: 26–41.

Woods, Tom. "Long-Range Planning for Seed Savers Exchange: Campout Speech by Tom Woods." *Harvest Edition*, 2001: 43–54.

———. Presentation at the 1985 Seed Conference, Missouri Botanical Gardens, St. Louis, Missouri. October 4–6, 1985. Reprinted in "Tom Woods," *Harvest Edition*, 1985: 51–54.

INDEX

Page numbers in **bold** indicate illustrations.

ILLUSTRATION CREDITS

The front jacket illustration for *Gathering* was originally created for the *Seed Savers 1994 Summer Edition* by our dear friend Judith Ann Griffith. For thirty years, her beautiful drawings and watercolors have graced the covers of Seed Savers Exchange publications. We are deeply grateful to Judith for granting permission to include reproductions of her work on pages iii, v–viii, xii, 7, 8, 21, 24, 26, 28, 30, 34, 38, 41, 42, 46, 66, 89, 96, 133, 136, 140, 143, 149, 180, 185, 190, 202, 206, 211, 214, 220, 223, 227, 232, and 244, plus the endsheets.

Photographer, botanist, and gardener David Cavagnaro has brought the beauty and bounty of Seed Savers Exchange before the eyes of the world through his exquisite photography. David's photographs have frequently appeared in SSE publications through the years. Once again he has generously permitted us to reproduce his work on pages 4, 33, 83, 92, 103, 121, 122, 126, 134, 165, 173, and 175–178.

Thanks to many other individuals and organizations for allowing us to use their photographic works: Penny Blazey, 167; Judy Blunk-Brawley/Becky Blunk-Silva, 47 (top); Larsh Bristol, 189; Rosalind Creasy, 70, 71, 197; Wil Davis, 139; Mike Day, 85, 95; Mark Fox, 62, 84; Tom Goodmann, 168; Jerry Johnson, 91, 99; Jeanne Malmgren, 64; Milwaukee Public Museum/Sumner W. Matteson Collection, 113, 116; Hilde Petersen, 196; Chip Peterson, 110; David Russell/The Martha Stewart Show, 163; K. Sahin, Zaden B.V., 156; Winneshiek County Historical Society/Colonel John W. Taylor Collection, 114.

Photographs from the Ott Whealy family collection appear on pages 2, 10, 12, 15, 19, 31, 51, 52, 56–61, 68, 77, 79, 144, 193–195, and 199.

Photographs taken by Seed Savers staff members are included on pages 47 (bottom), 105, 108, 129, 151, 153, 154, 159, 171, 198, 201, 204, 217, 228, 230, and 231.

SEED SAVERS EXCHANGE

Seed Savers Exchange (SSE) was founded in 1975 by Diane Ott Whealy and Kent Whealy after Diane's terminally ill grandfather entrusted them with garden seeds brought by his parents from Bavaria. Grandpa Ott's morning glory and German Pink tomato inspired the Whealys to search for other gardeners growing heirloom seeds.

Seed Savers Exchange is the preeminent nonprofit seed-saving organization in the United States. Its mission is to help preserve our diverse, but endangered, garden heritage for future generations by building a network of people committed to collecting, conserving, and sharing heirloom seeds and plants, while educating people about the value of genetic and cultural diversity.

This "participatory preservation" effort has grown from a handful of people collecting and distributing seeds into a network of more than thirteen thousand members. Seed Savers Exchange is headquartered at Heritage Farm near Decorah, Iowa, where it maintains a collection of thousands of heirloom and open-pollinated varieties of vegetables, herbs, fruits, and flowers. SSE also maintains a herd of Ancient White Park cattle.

Proceeds from the sale of *Gathering* will support
Seed Savers Exchange's nonprofit mission.
Visit us at www.seedsavers.org

Seed Savers Exchange
3094 North Winn Road
Decorah, Iowa 52101
(563) 382-5990

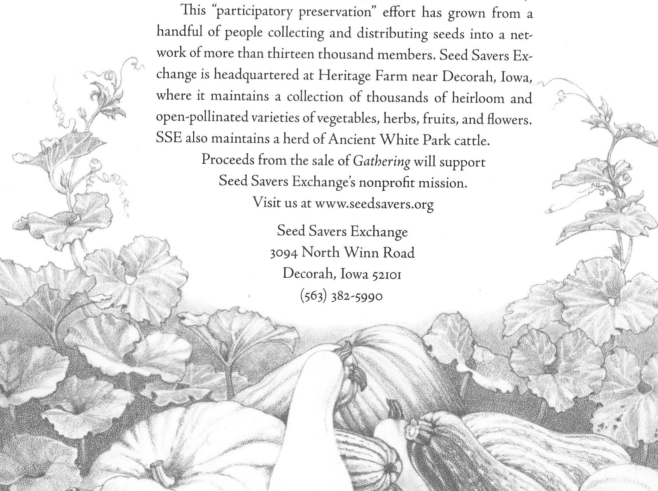